Invertebrates
of the
Puget Sound Region
Coloring Book

Zoe Powell

This book is dedicated to all the backyard biologists, young and old.

ISBN-13:9781546473480

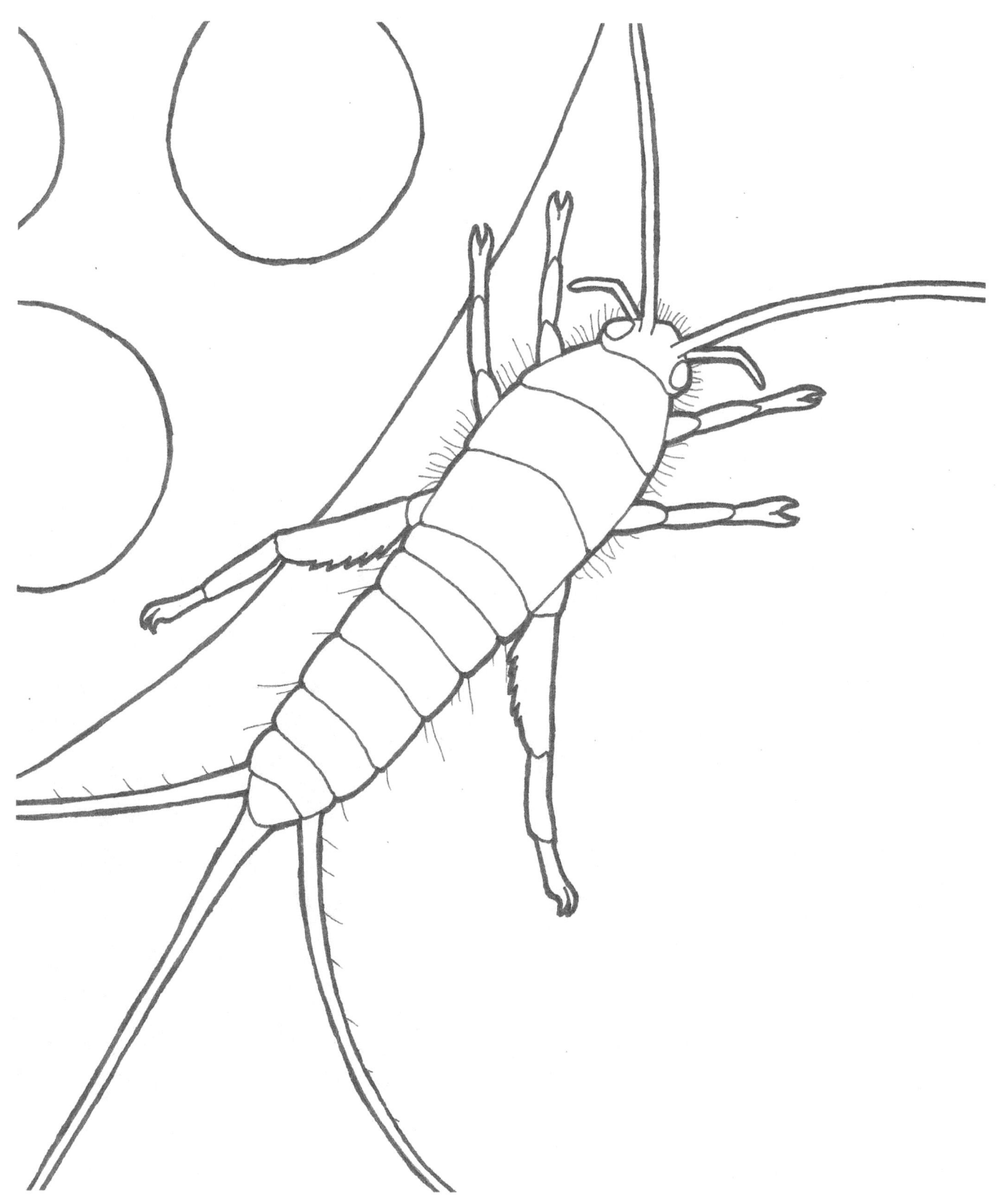

Silverfish

These harmless insects are often found stuck in sinks and bathtubs.

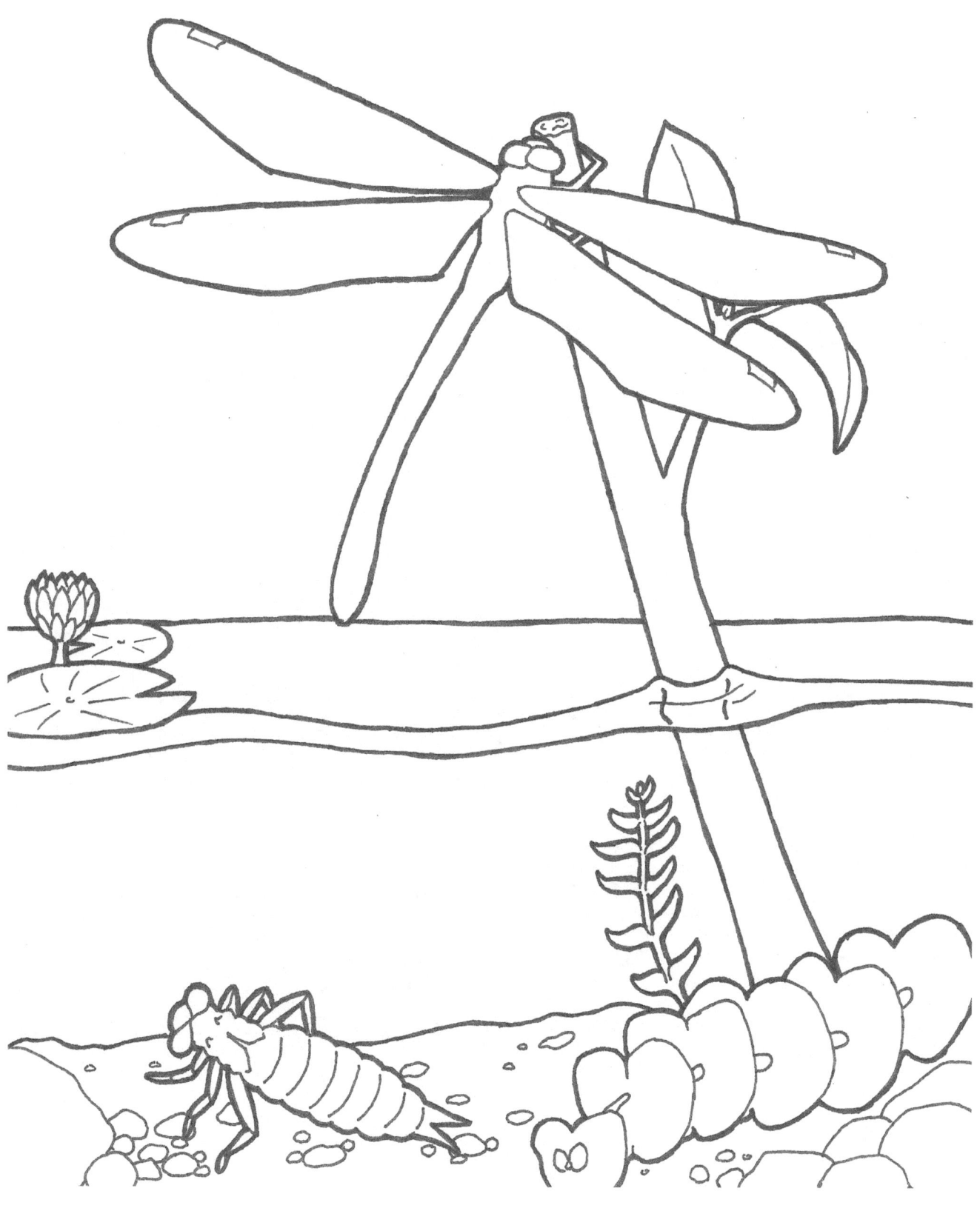

Dragonfly

Dragonflies eat mosquitoes and other small flies. They start life as larvae living underwater.

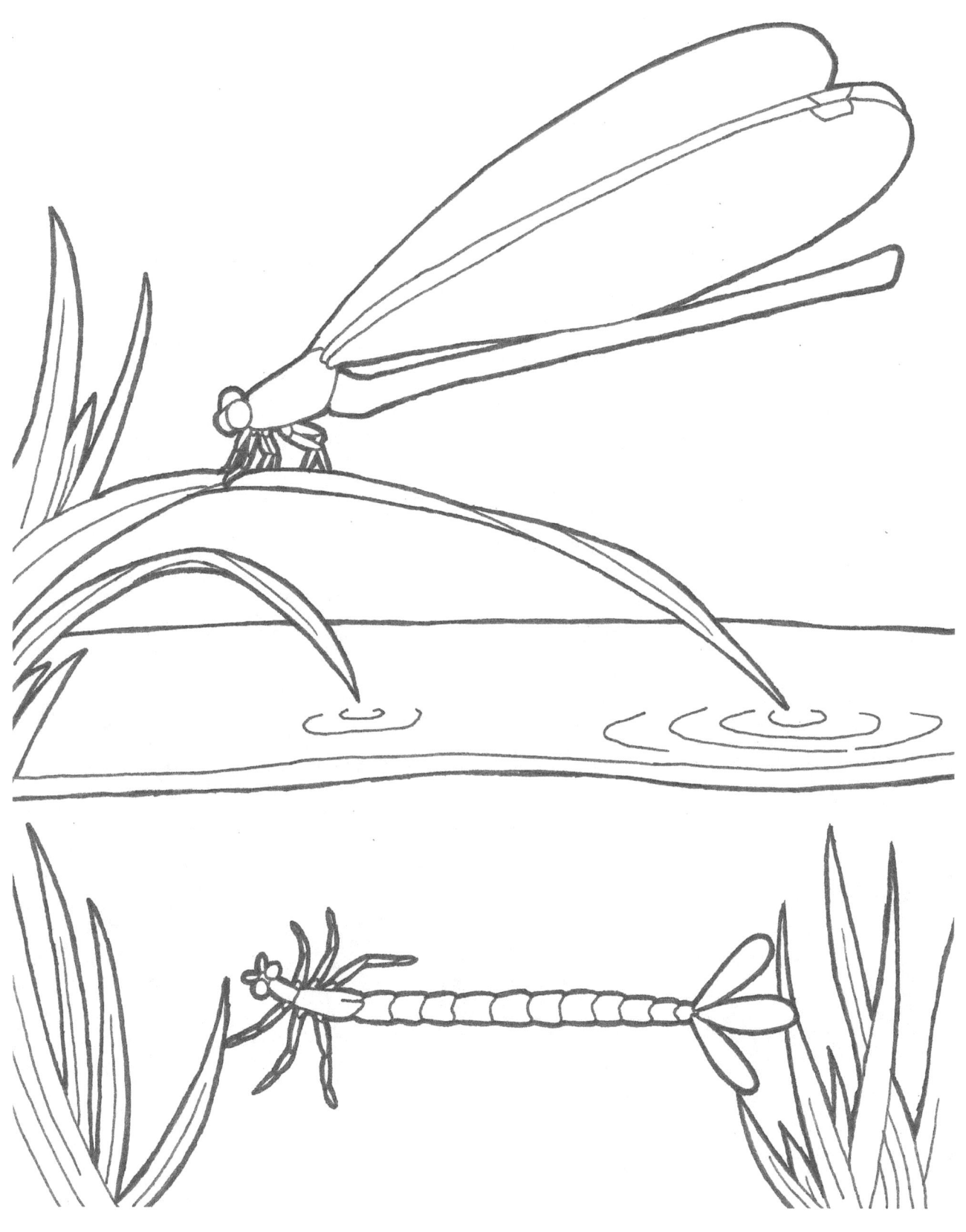

Damselfly

Damselflies are very similar to dragonflies, but their wings fold up behind them
when they rest.

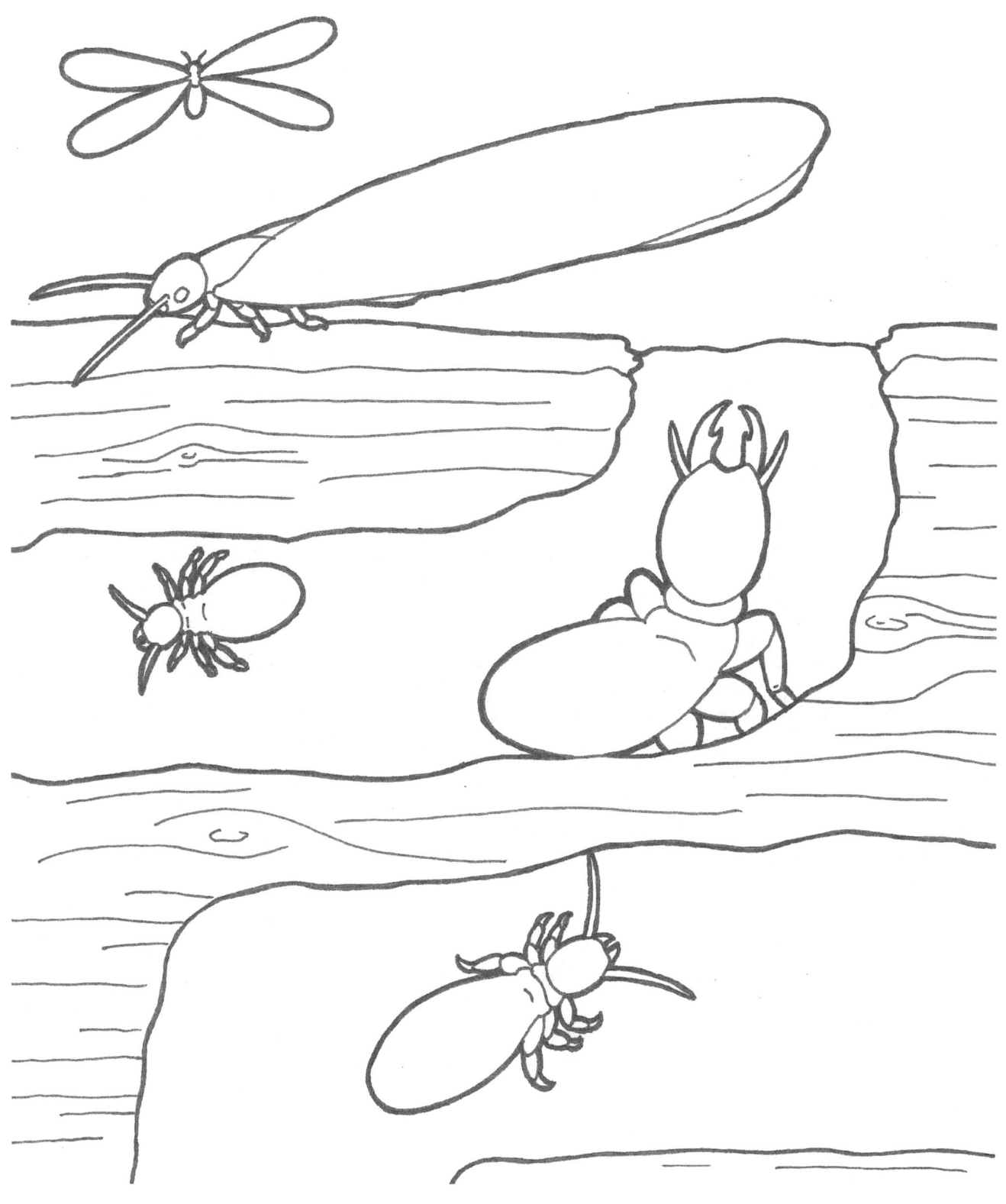

Termites

Termites live in tunnels dug in rotten wood or built of mud. They have several kinds in each nest including: a queen, winged adults, guards, and workers.

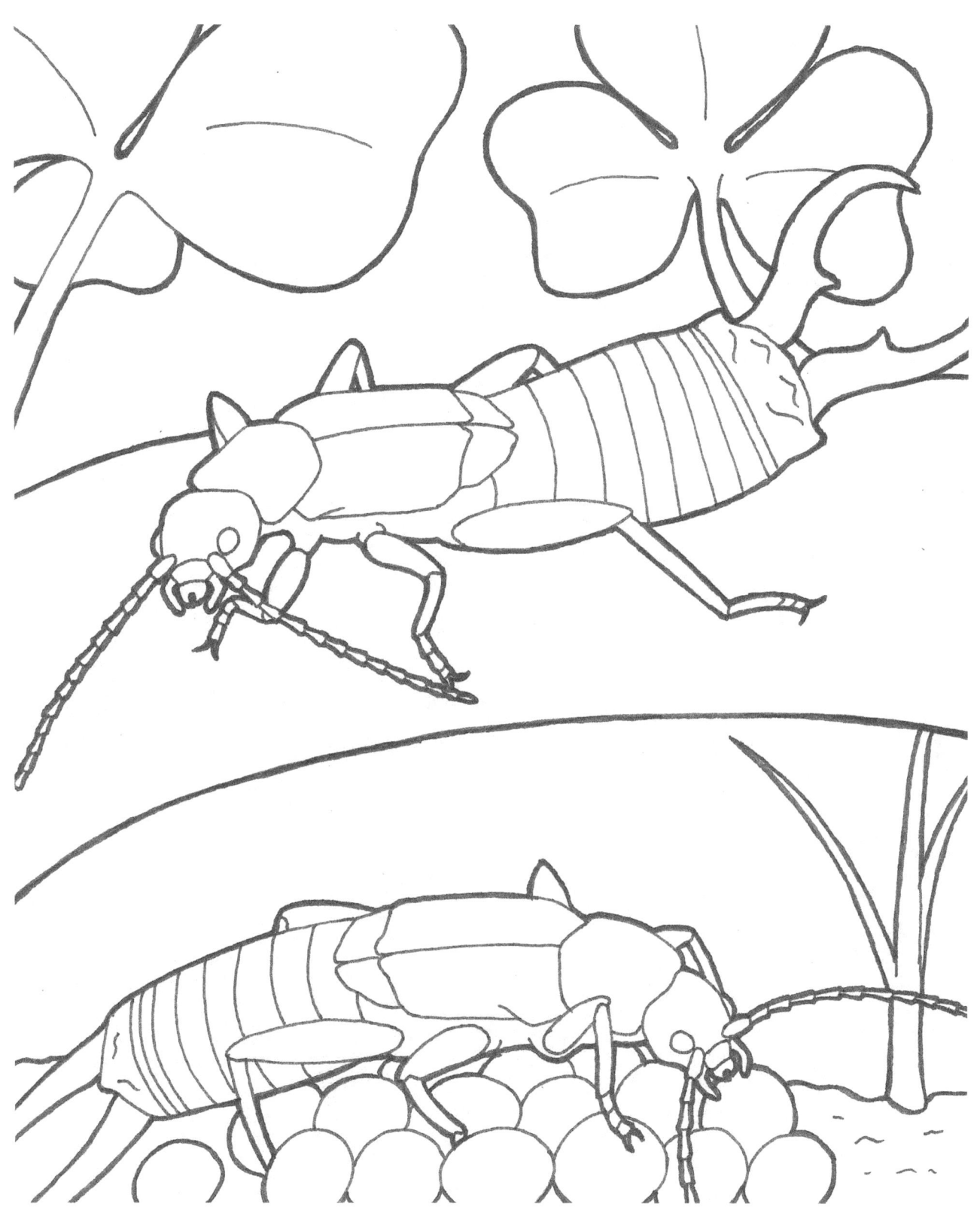

Earwigs

Earwigs do not try to crawl in peoples' ears. Amazingly, the females often take very good care of their eggs and babies.

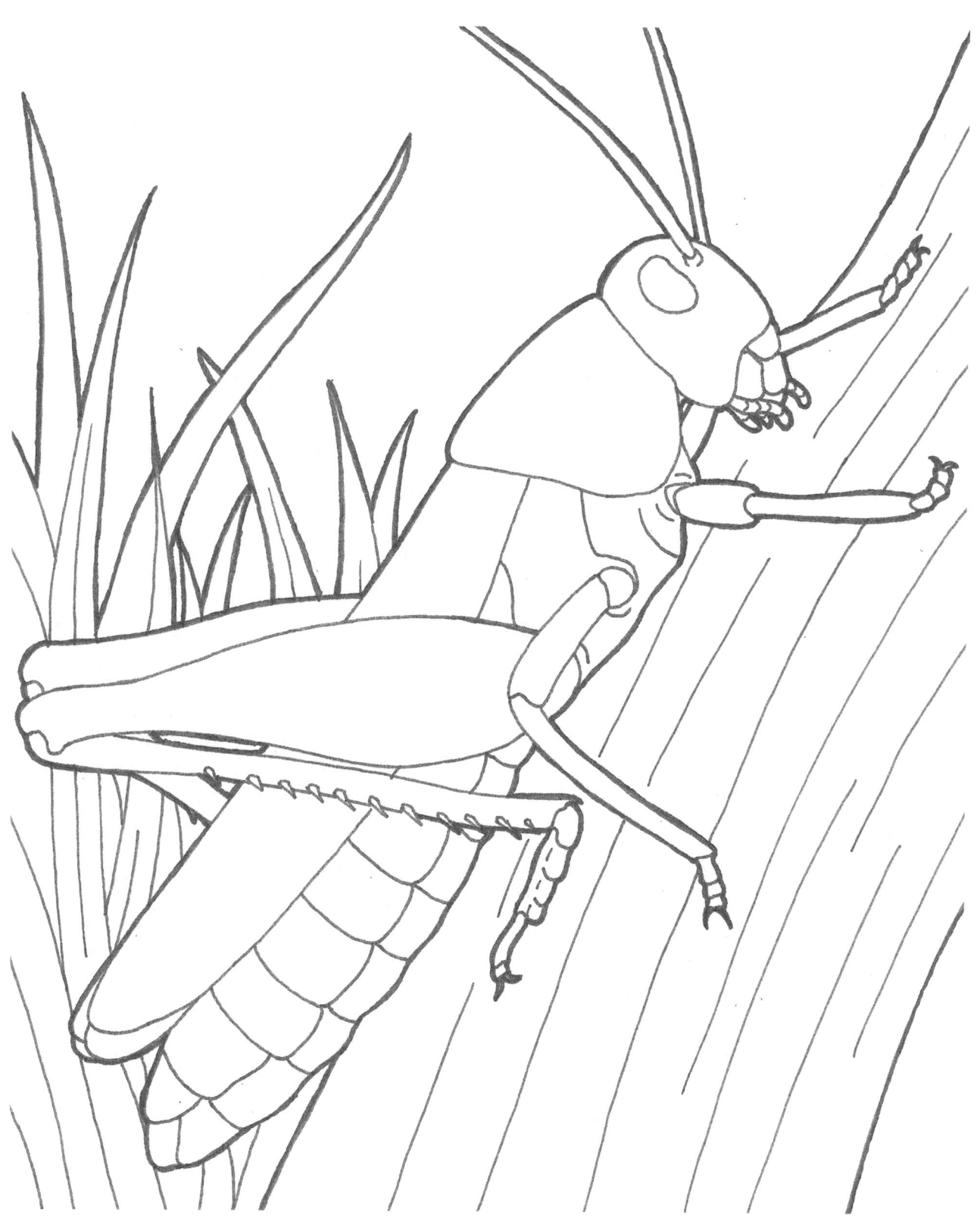

Grasshopper

Grasshoppers like to eat grasses and leaves. They are most commonly found in fields or sometimes on lawns.

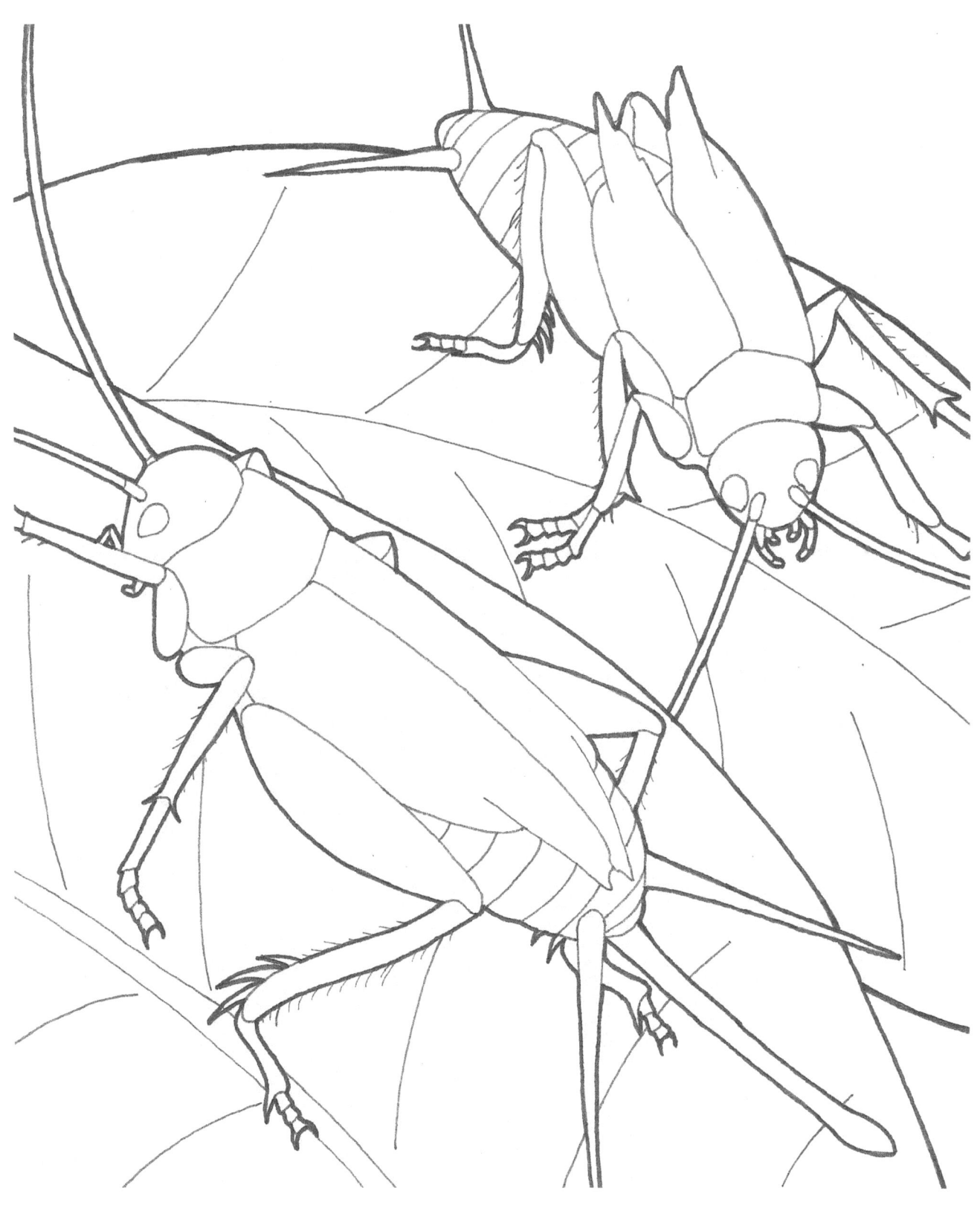

Crickets

Male crickets use their wings to make a loud chirping noise. Female crickets have a long egg-laying tube called an ovipositor.

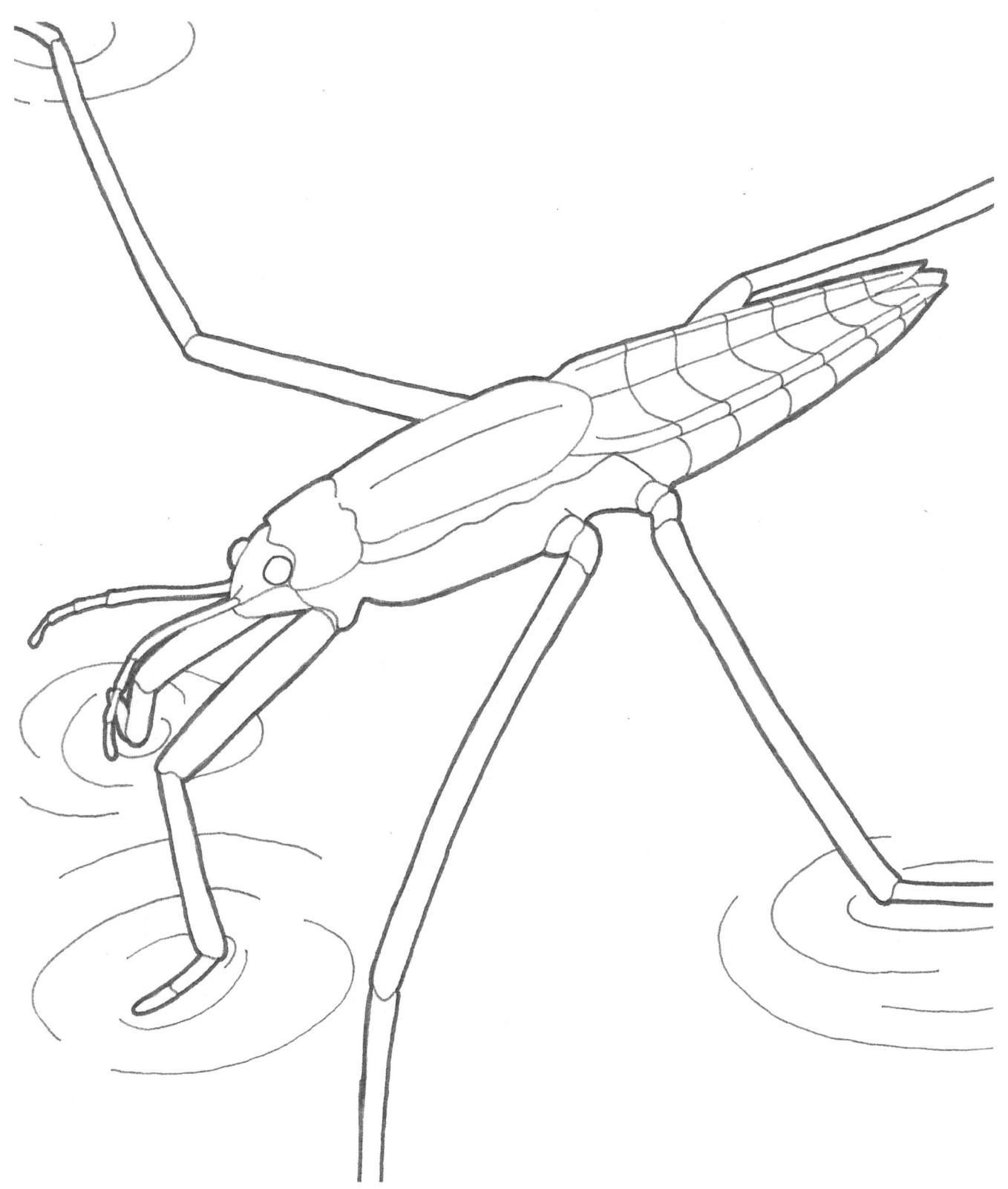

Water Strider

Water striders live on the surface of ponds and pools in streams. They hunt insects that have been trapped by the water's surface.

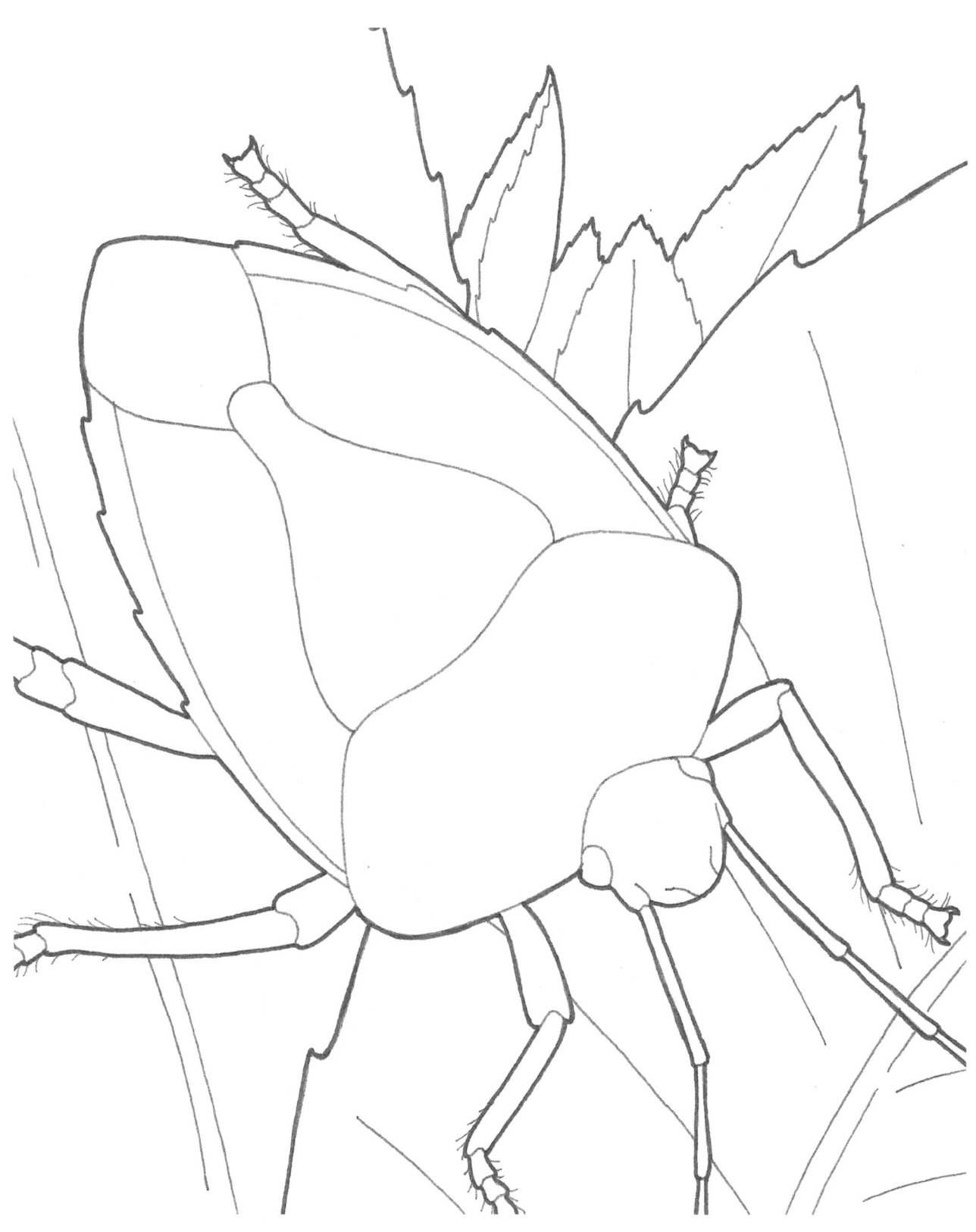

Stink Bug

As their name suggests, stink bugs produce a yucky smell when threatened. They feed on plants.

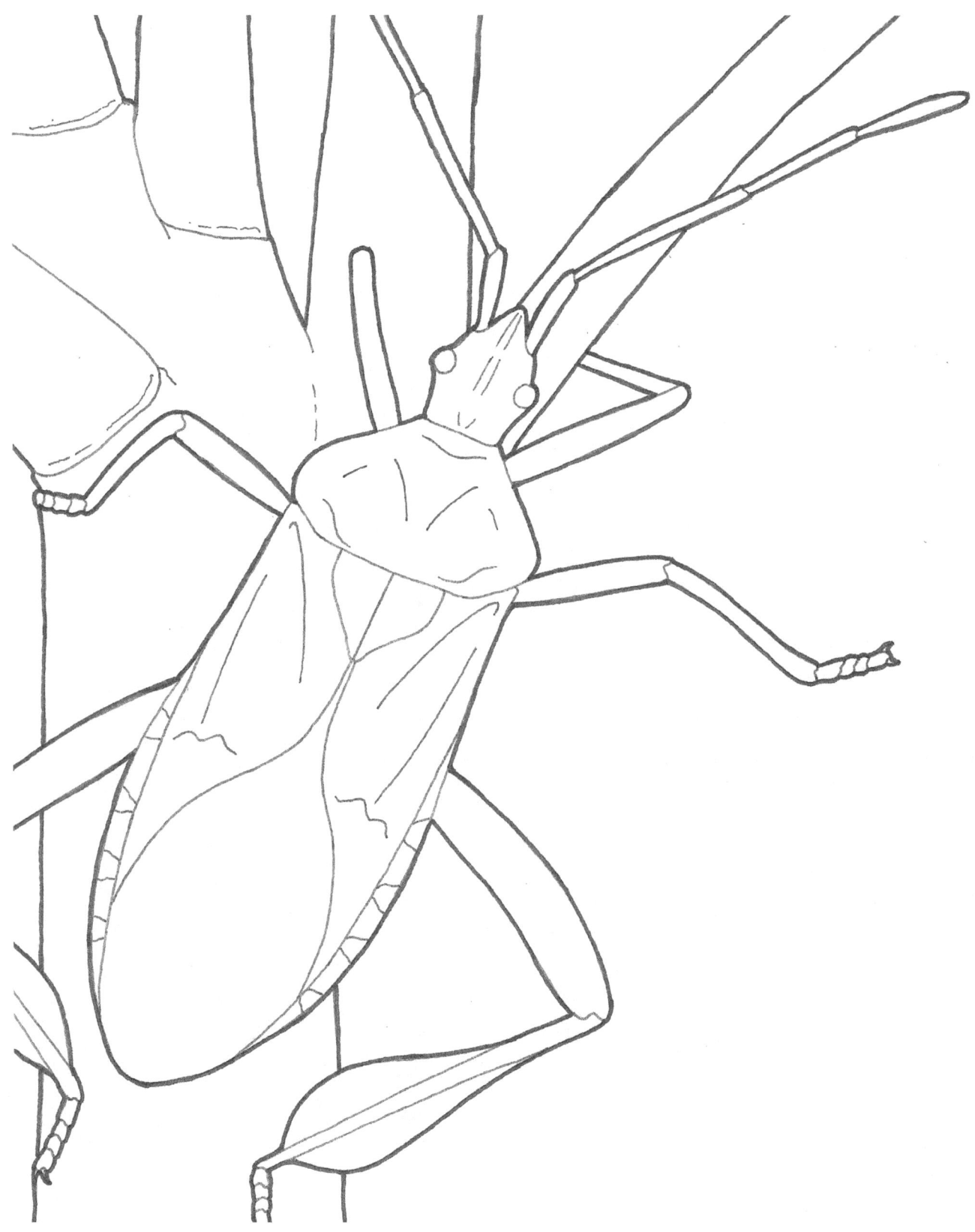

Western Conifer Seed Bug

These bugs primarily feed on the seeds and cones of conifer trees. They can be found seeking warmth in houses in fall and early winter.

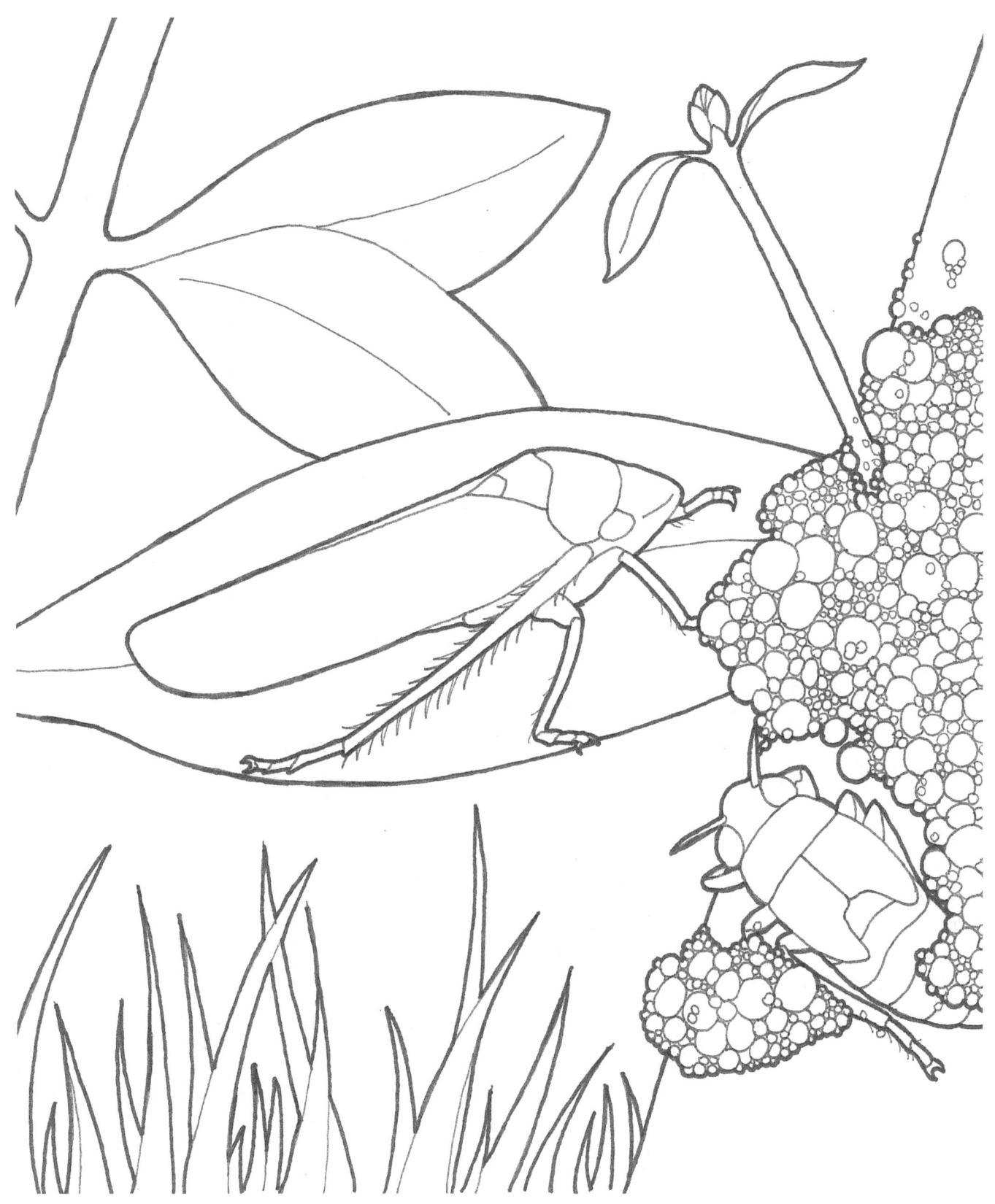

Leafhoppers

Leafhopper nymphs live in homes made of a spit-like foam. Nymphs and adults both eat sap from plants.

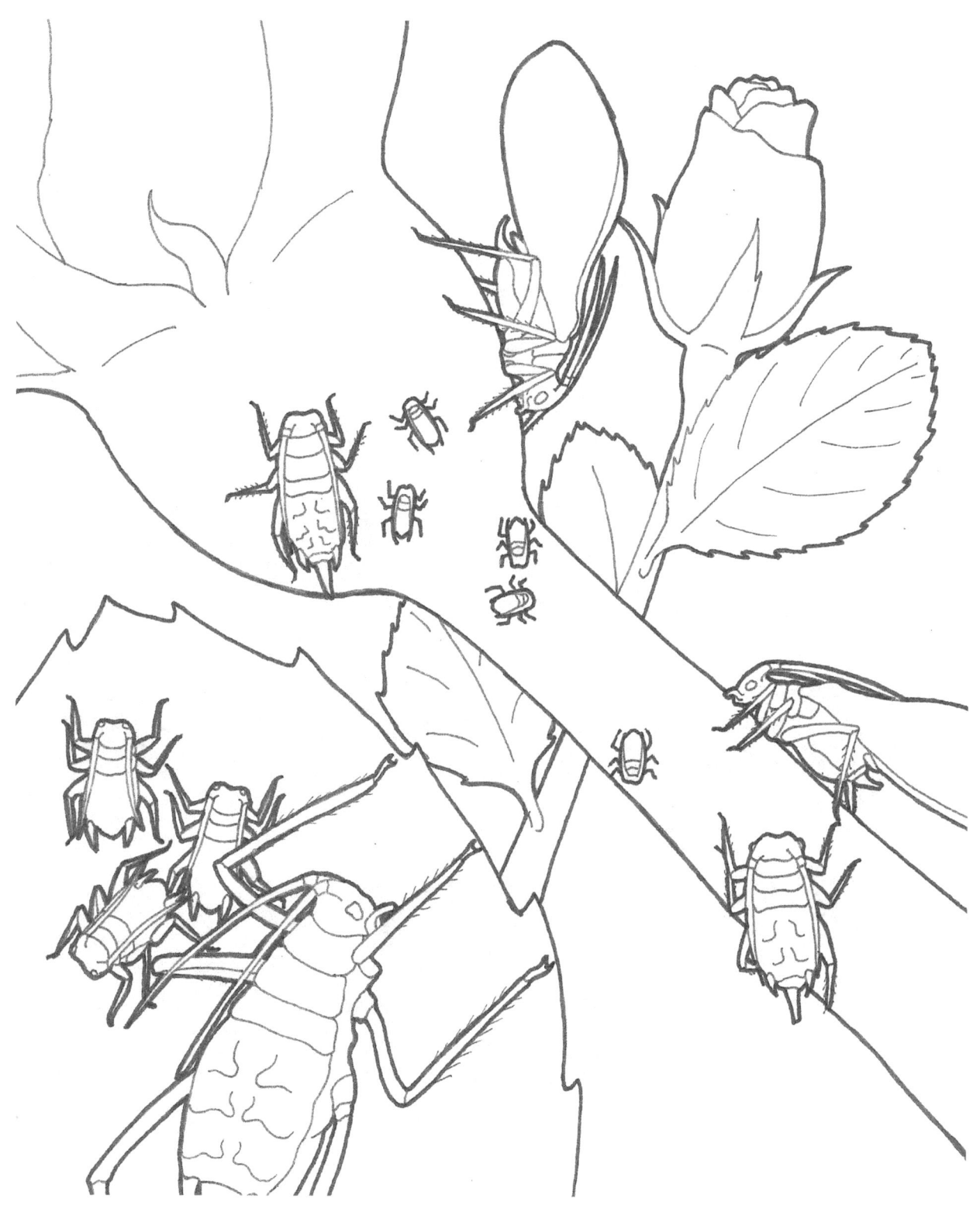

Aphids

Aphids are common garden pests that drink sap from plants. Winged adults may be male or female, but non-winged adults are always female. In every other generation in some species the females clone themselves.

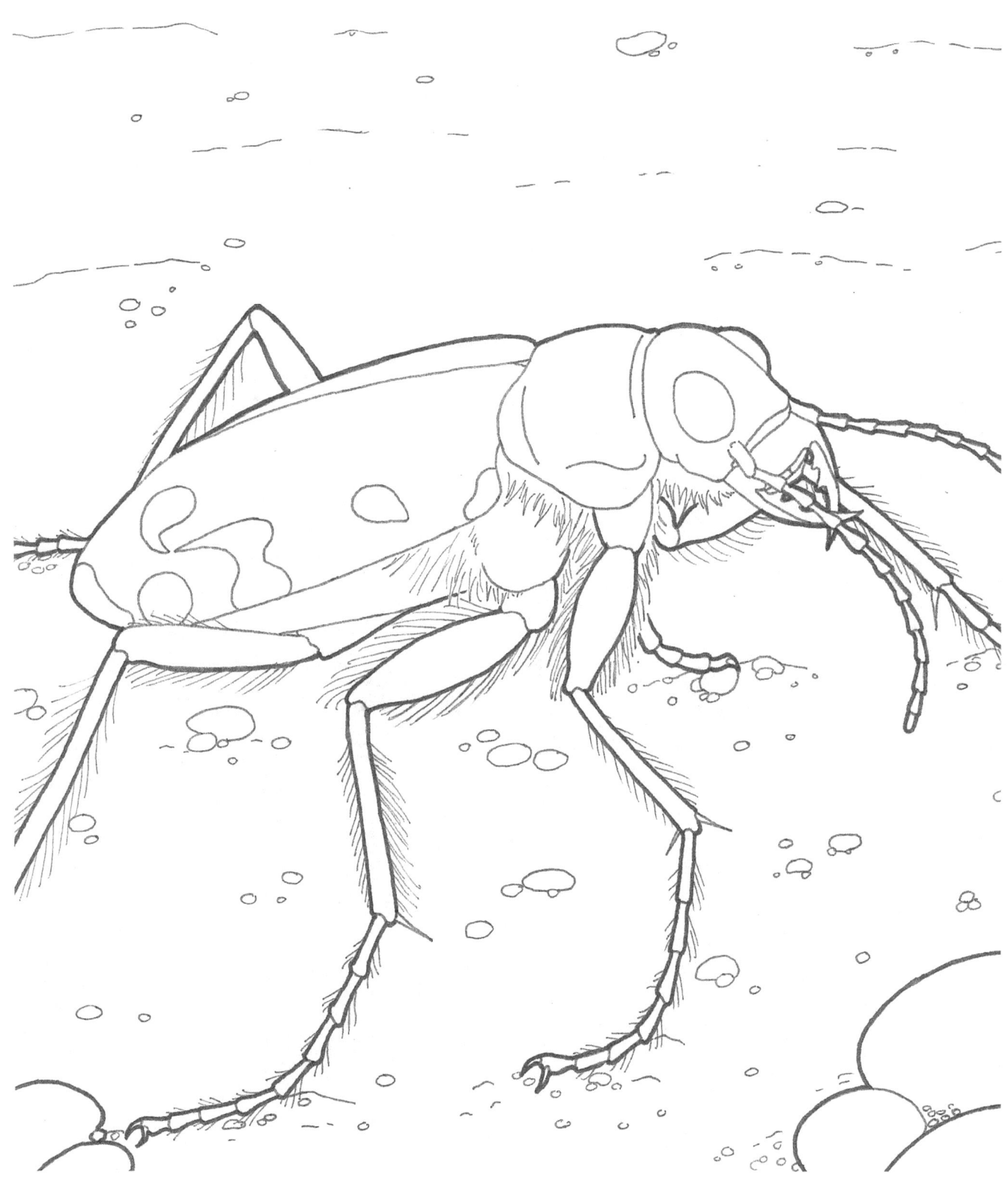

Tiger Beetle

Tiger beetles are fierce predators that can usually be found hunting on beaches and other sandy areas. Larvae live in burrows underground.

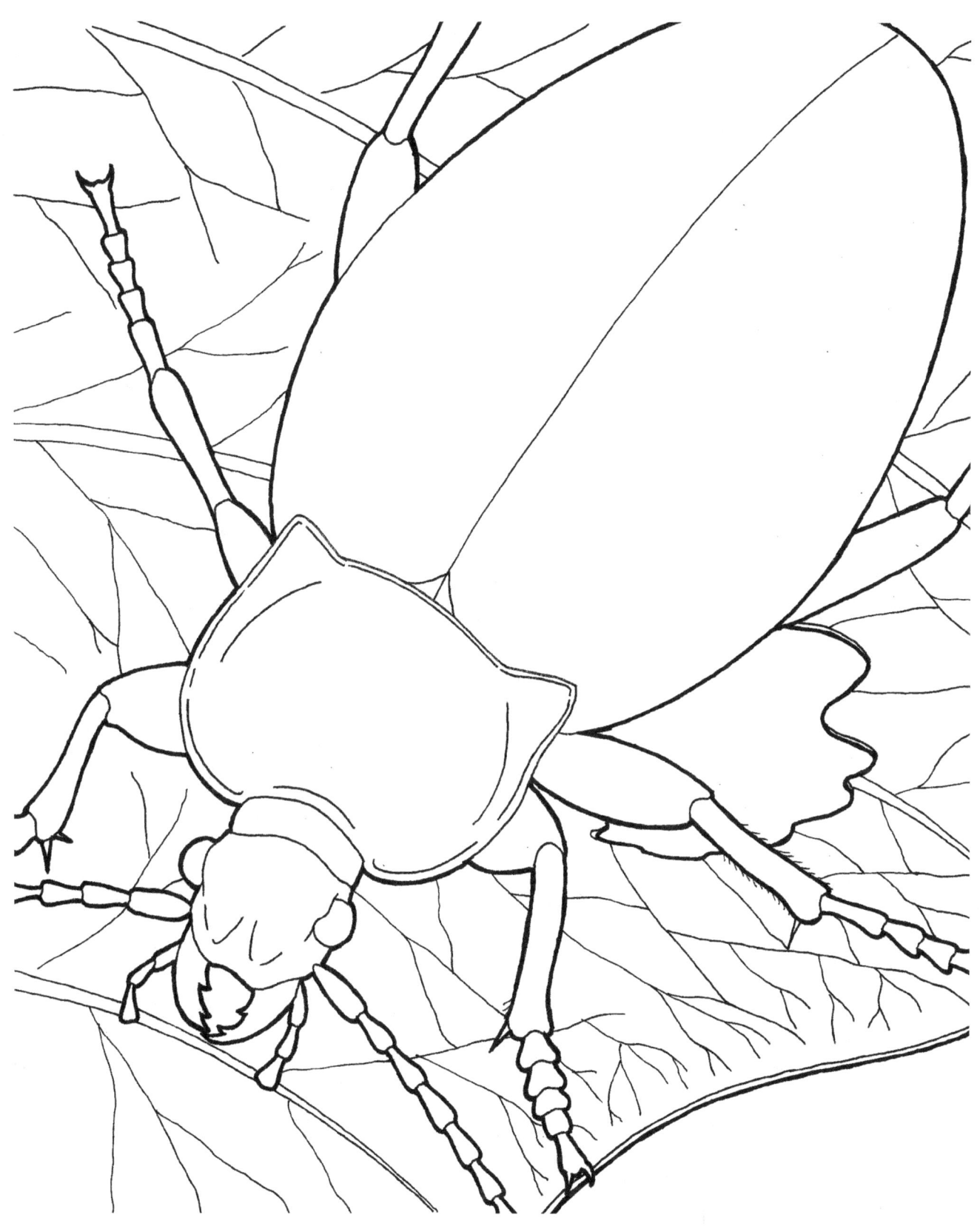

Ground Beetle

These beetles are commonly found in gardens and forests. They eat a variety of
soft-bodied animals like caterpillars and small slugs.

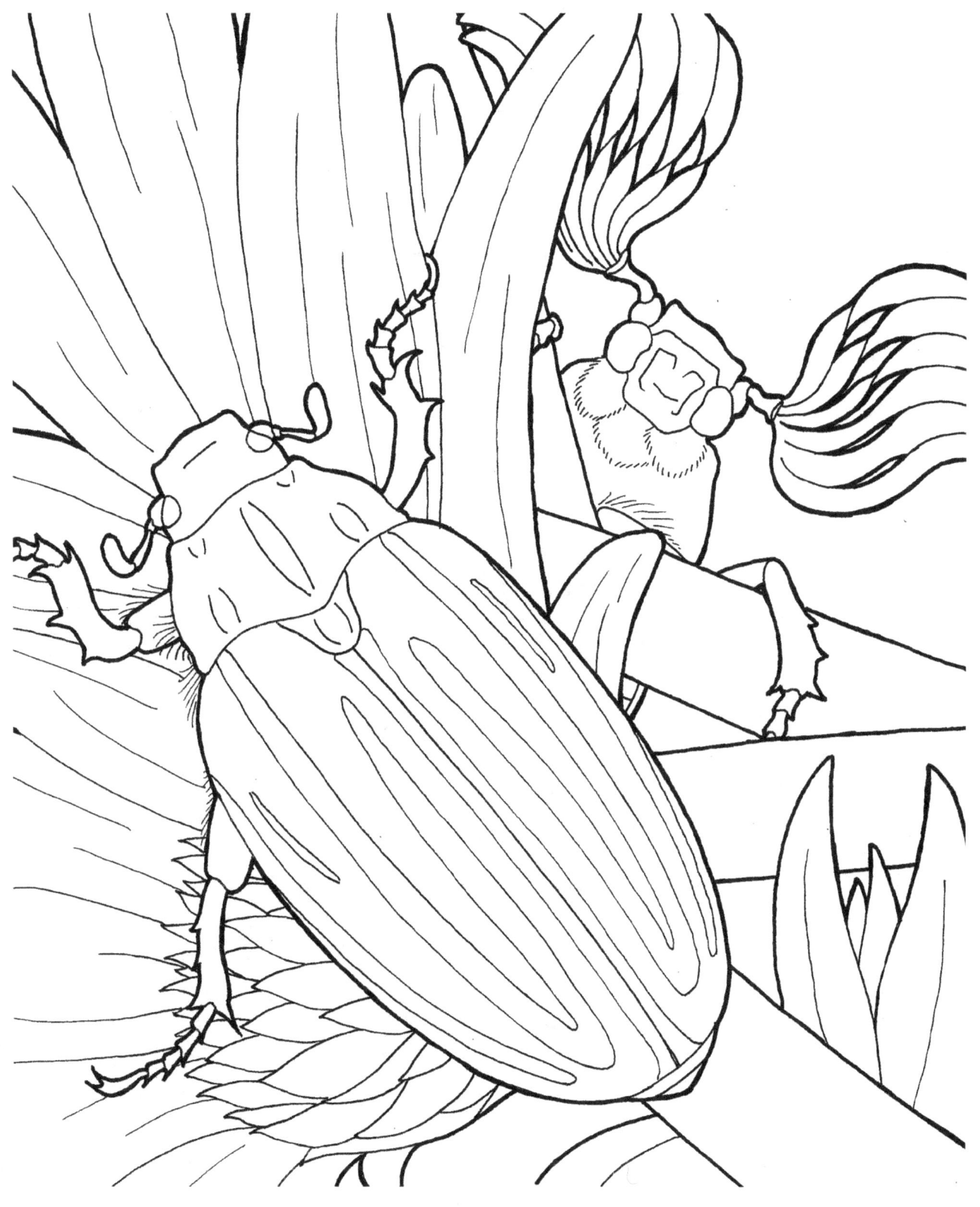

June Beetle

These large beetles are found in summer. The males have huge fan-like antennae. Despite their size, they can fly, though are usually seen crawling on plants or on the ground.

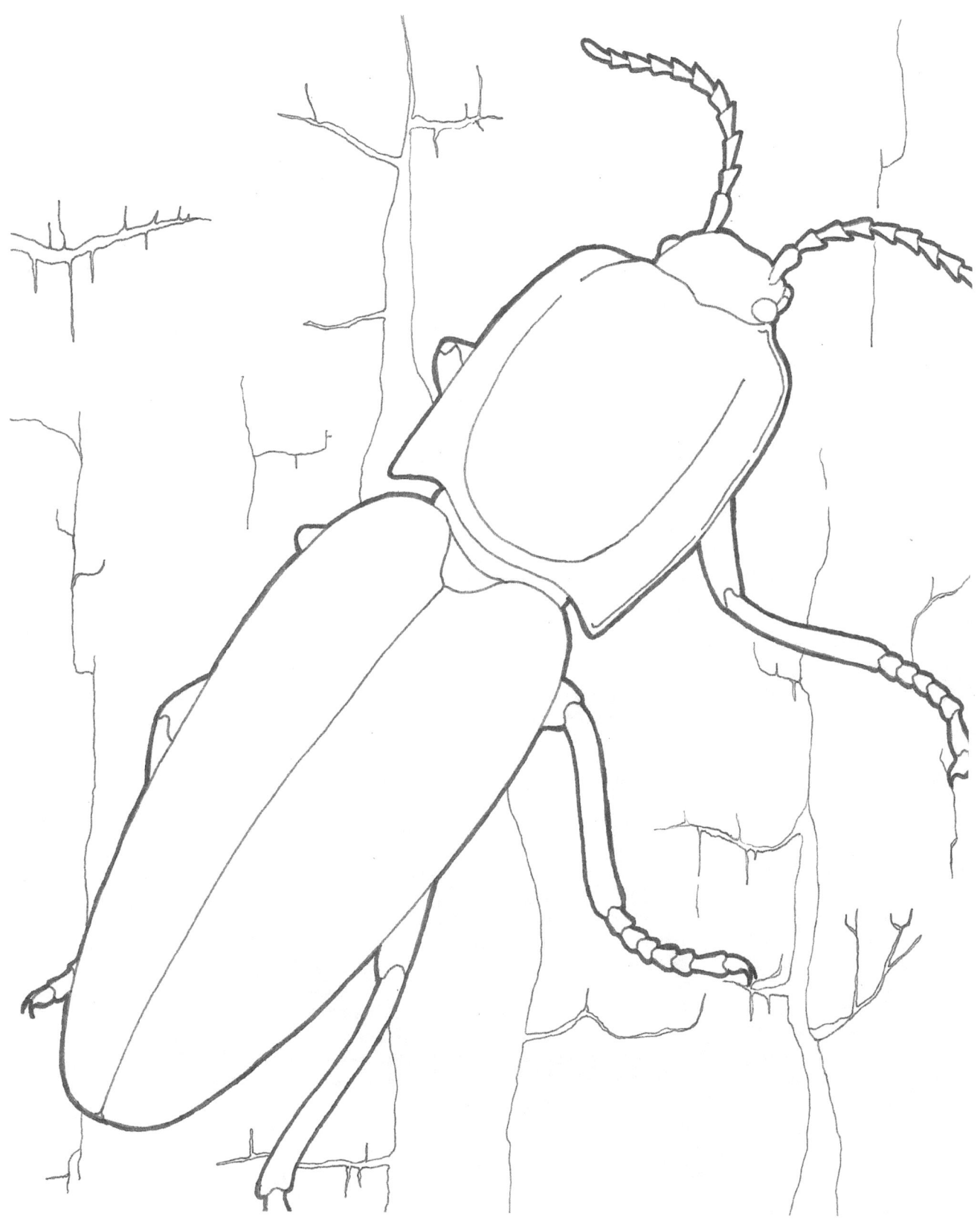

Click Beetle

Click beetles have special structures in their body that allow them to make a loud
clicking noise and fling themselves into the air to escape predators.

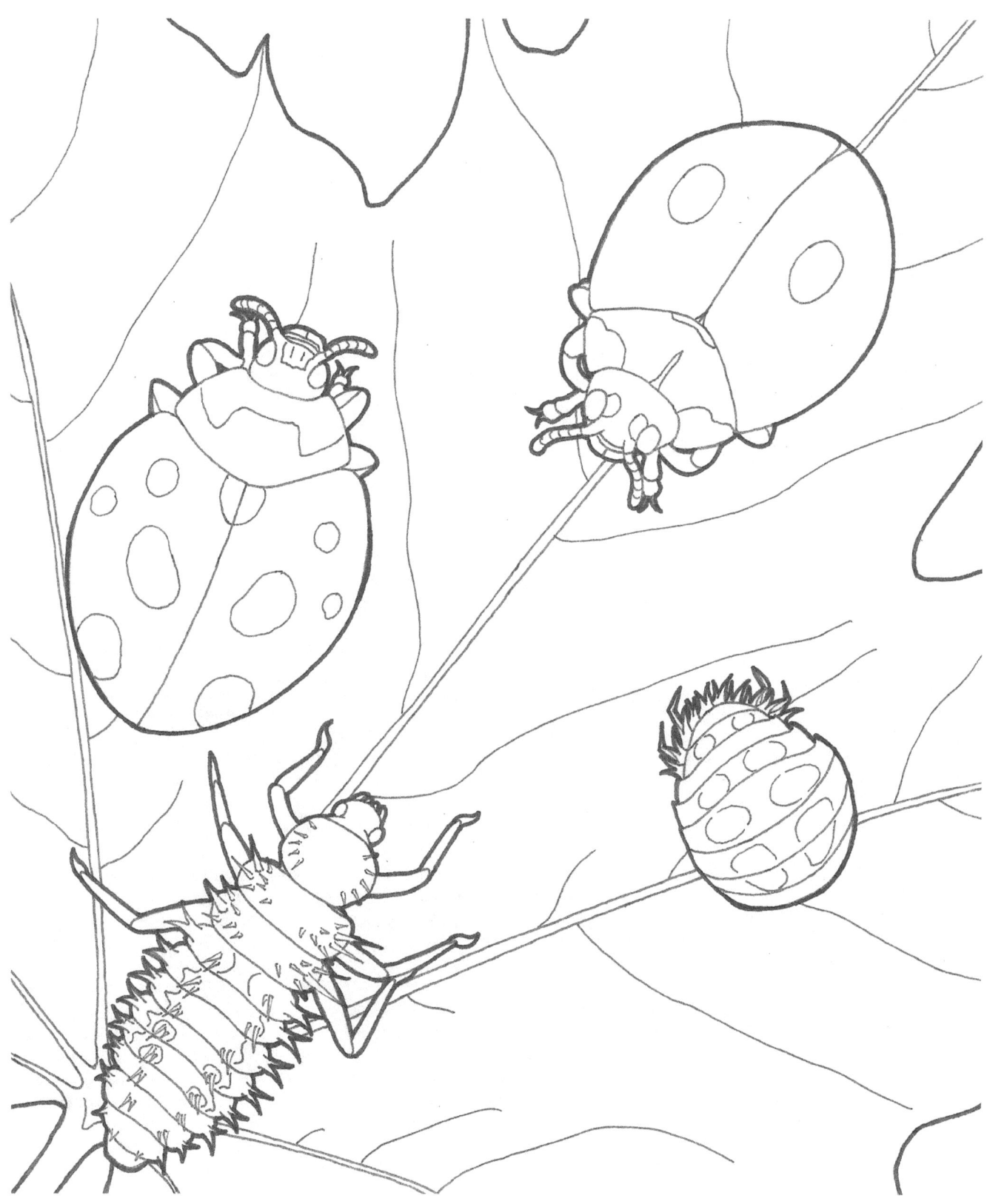

Lady Beetle

Like butterflies, lady beetles have three life stages: larvae, pupae, and adult. There are many species of lady beetle with different colors and patterns.

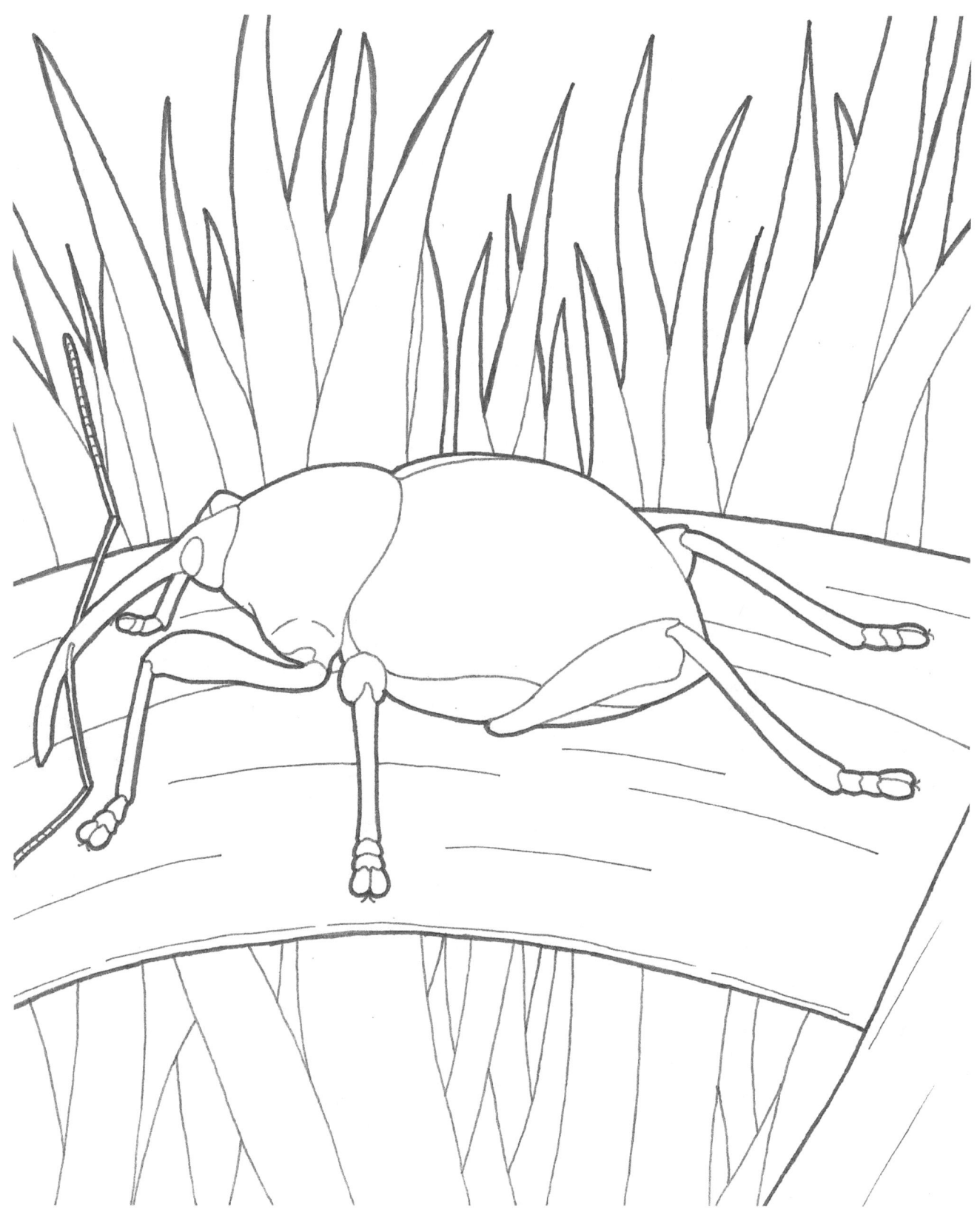

Weevil

There are many species of weevil. All eat plants, and some species are notorious pests eating grains and other crops. They are very small.

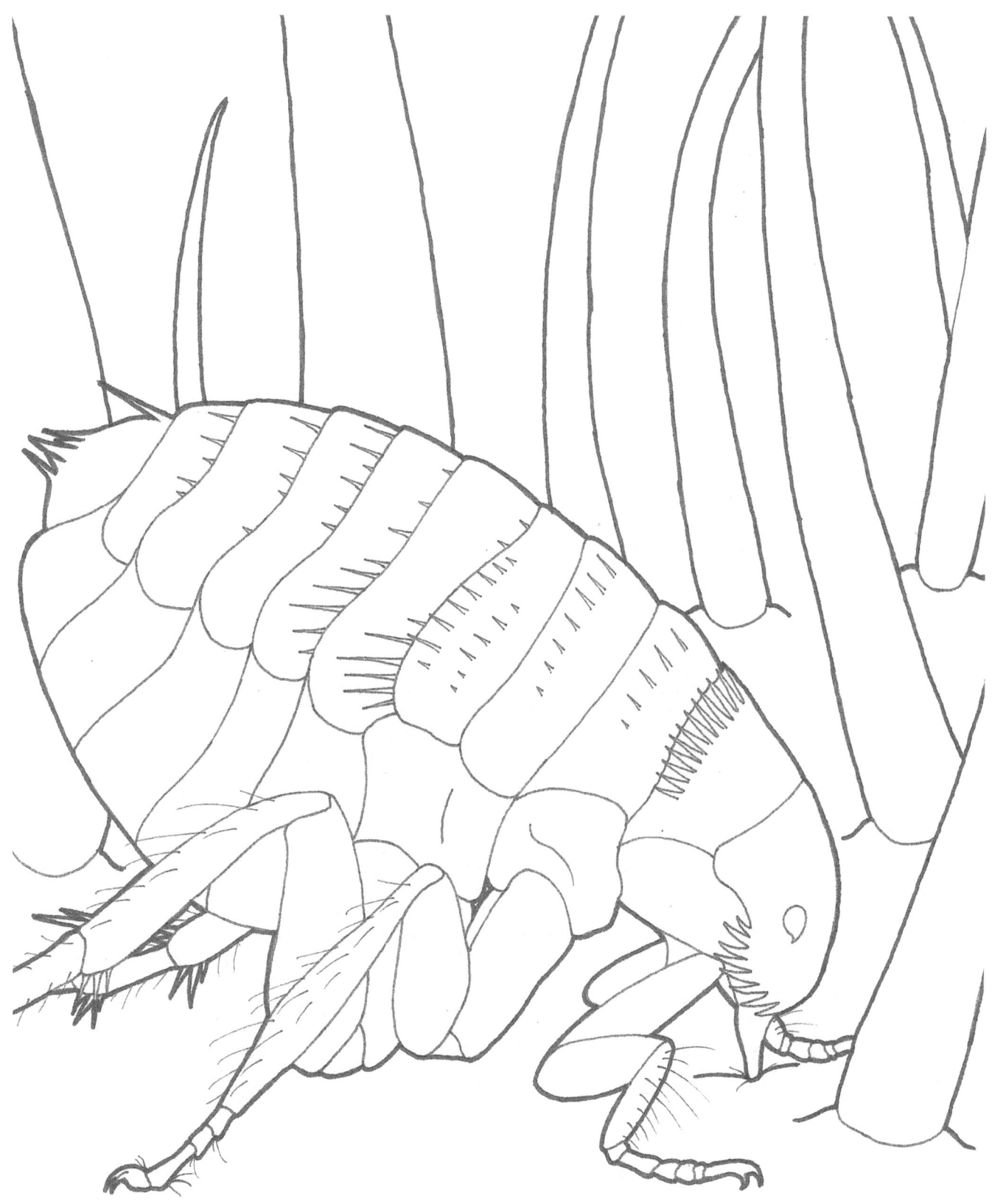

Flea

Fleas drink blood from their hosts. There are many different species of flea that each specialize in different hosts, including humans, dogs, and cats.

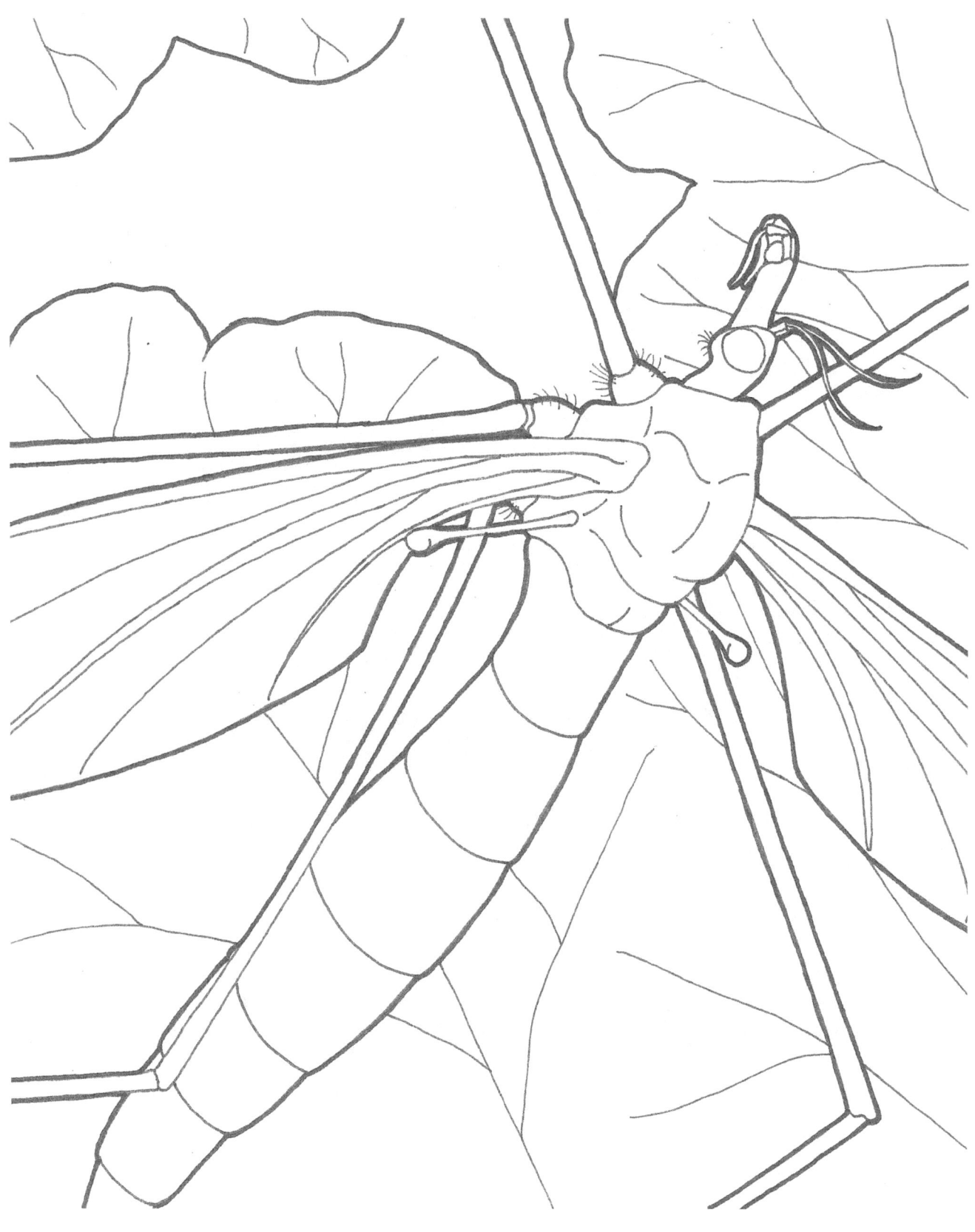

Crane Fly

Crane flies are harmless. Contrary to popular belief, they do not eat mosquitos. In fact, they may not eat at all!

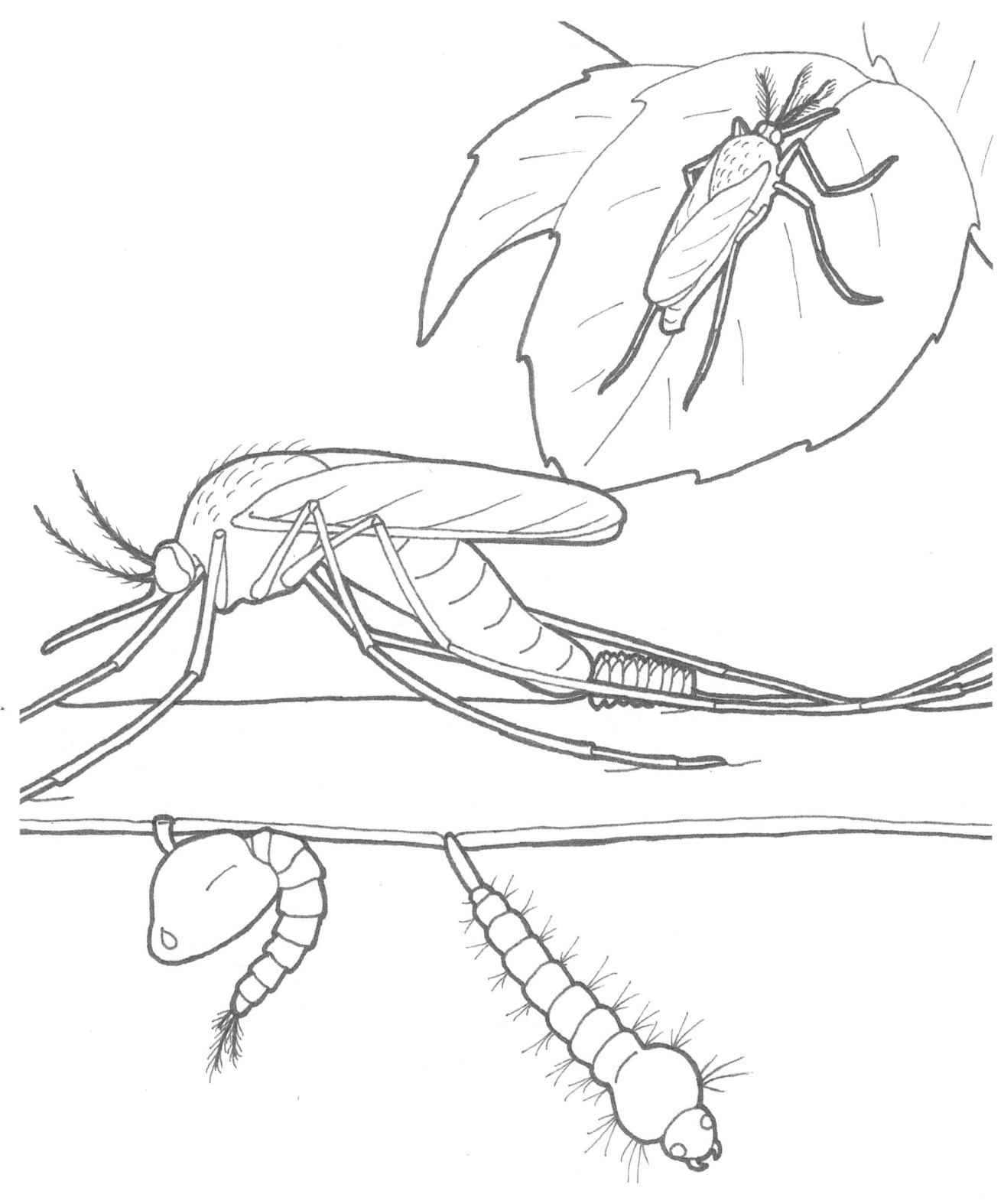

Mosquito

Only female mosquitos drink blood, males feed on nectar and sap from plants.
Both larval and pupa stages live in calm waters and can be found even in buckets
of water in yards.

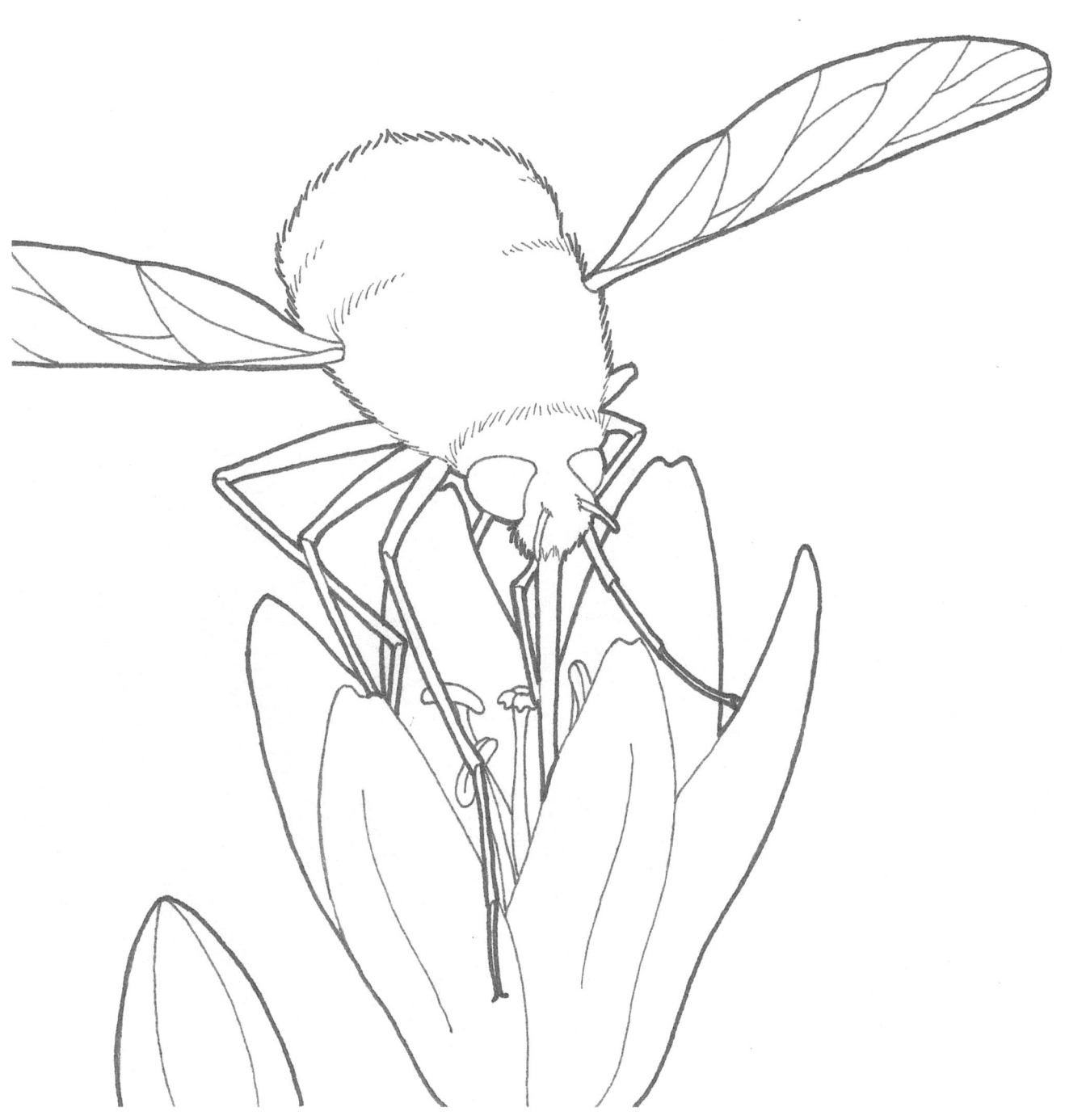

Bee Fly

These flies have evolved to look like bees in a process called mimicry. They don't have stingers, but since many bees do have stingers the flies are safer from predators when they look like bees.

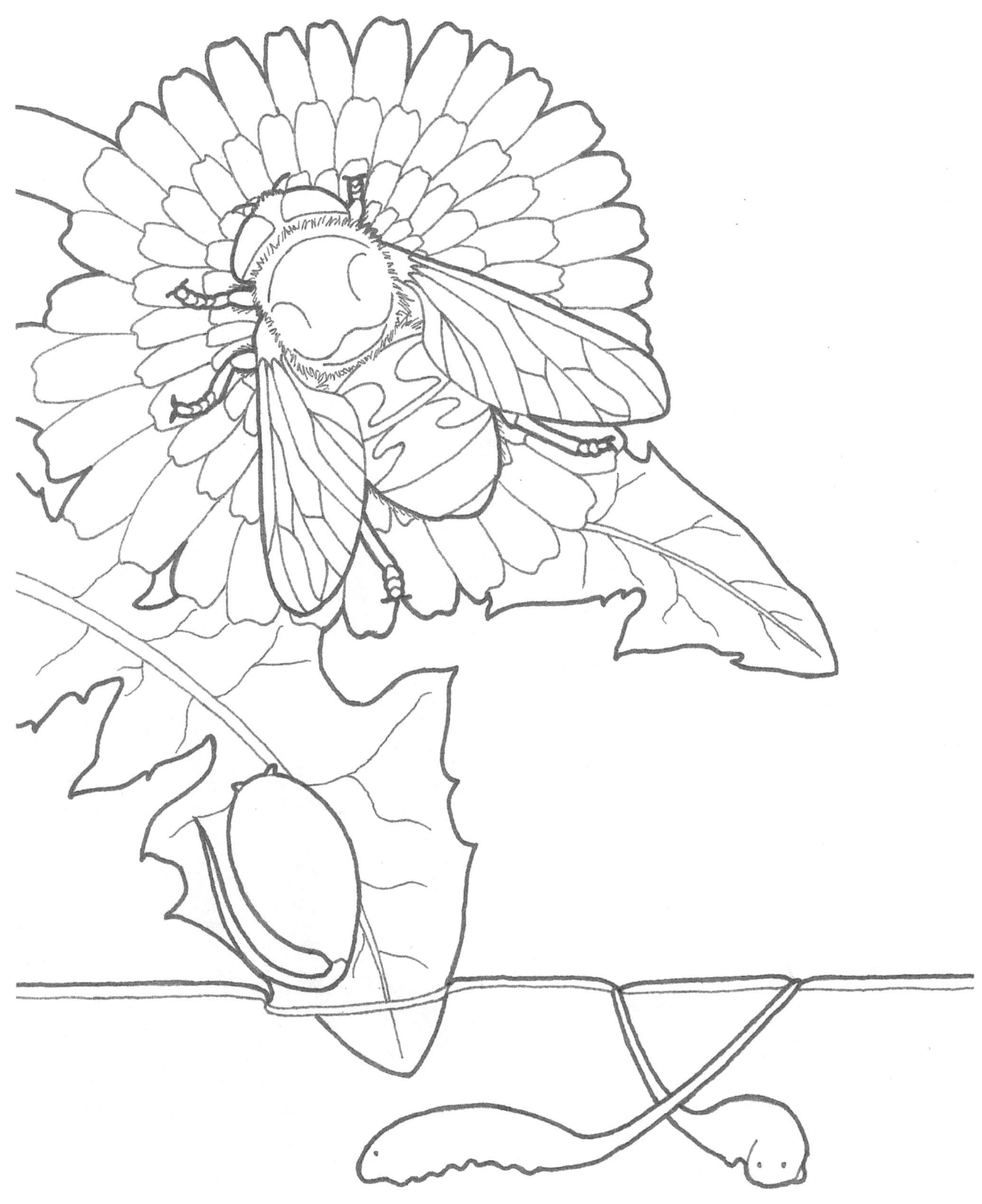

Drone Fly

These flies pollinate flowers and look like bees, but have wide heads and huge eyes. The larvae are called rat-tailed maggots and live in still, dirty water.

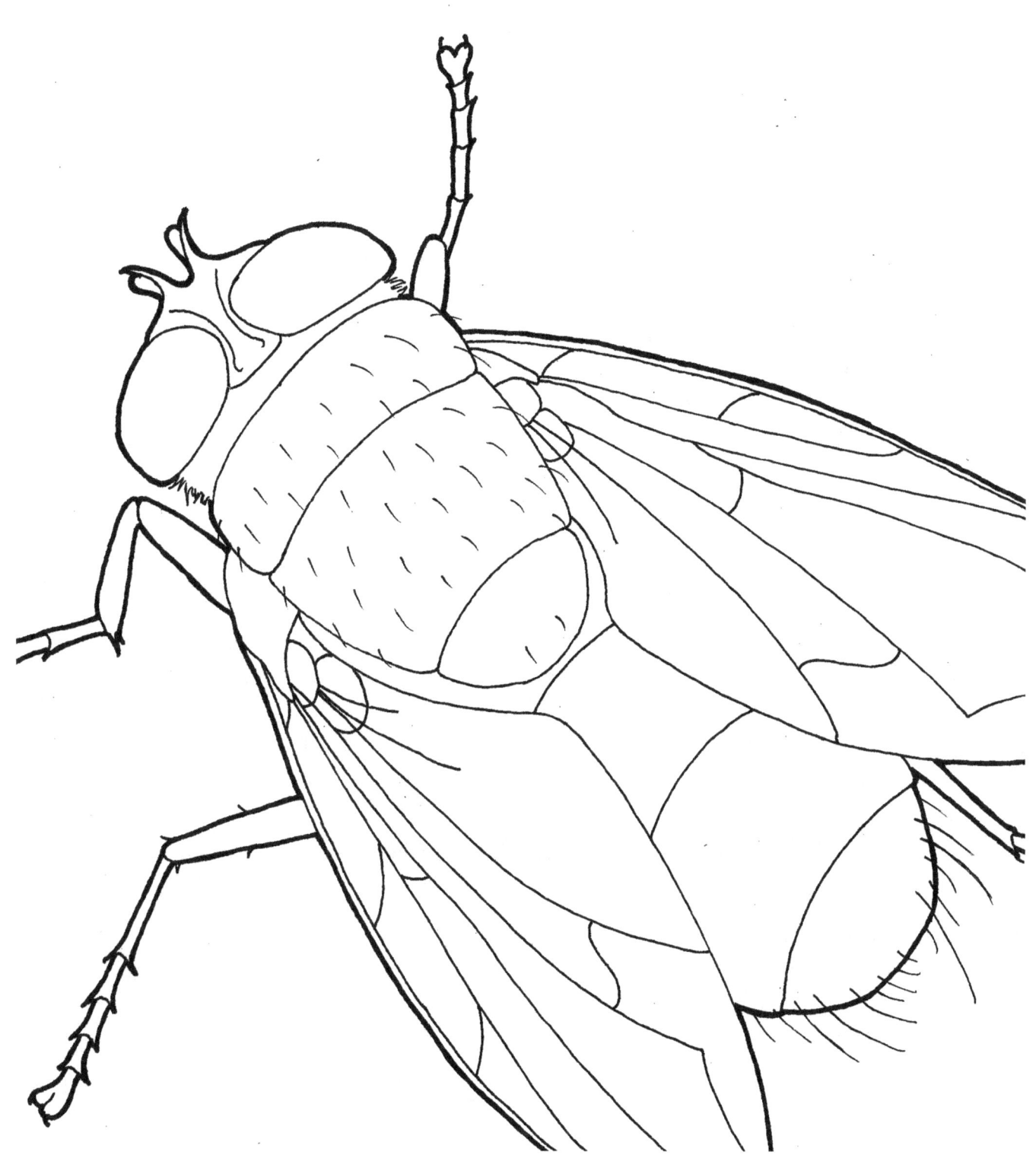

Green Bottle Fly

Commonly seen on warm sunny days, these flies feed on just about anything with liquids in it. Most famously, dog poop. Larva feed on rotting meat, and sterile ones are even bred for medical use in cleaning infected wounds.

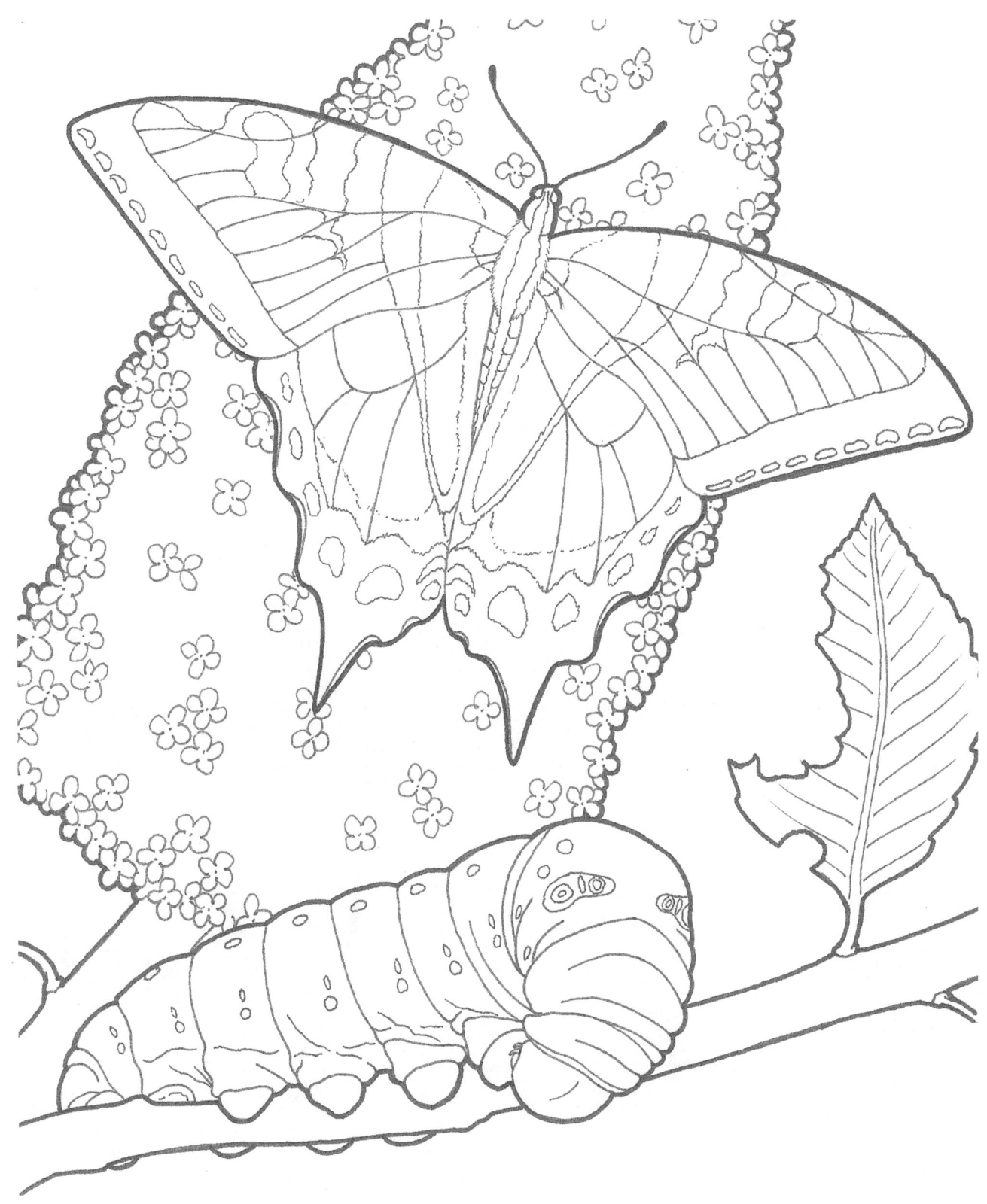

Western Tiger Swallowtail

The caterpillars have bright false eyespots on the hump behind their head,
probably to confuse predators. While the adults feed on a wide variety of flowers,
the larva only eat alders, aspens, willows, poplars, and sycamores.

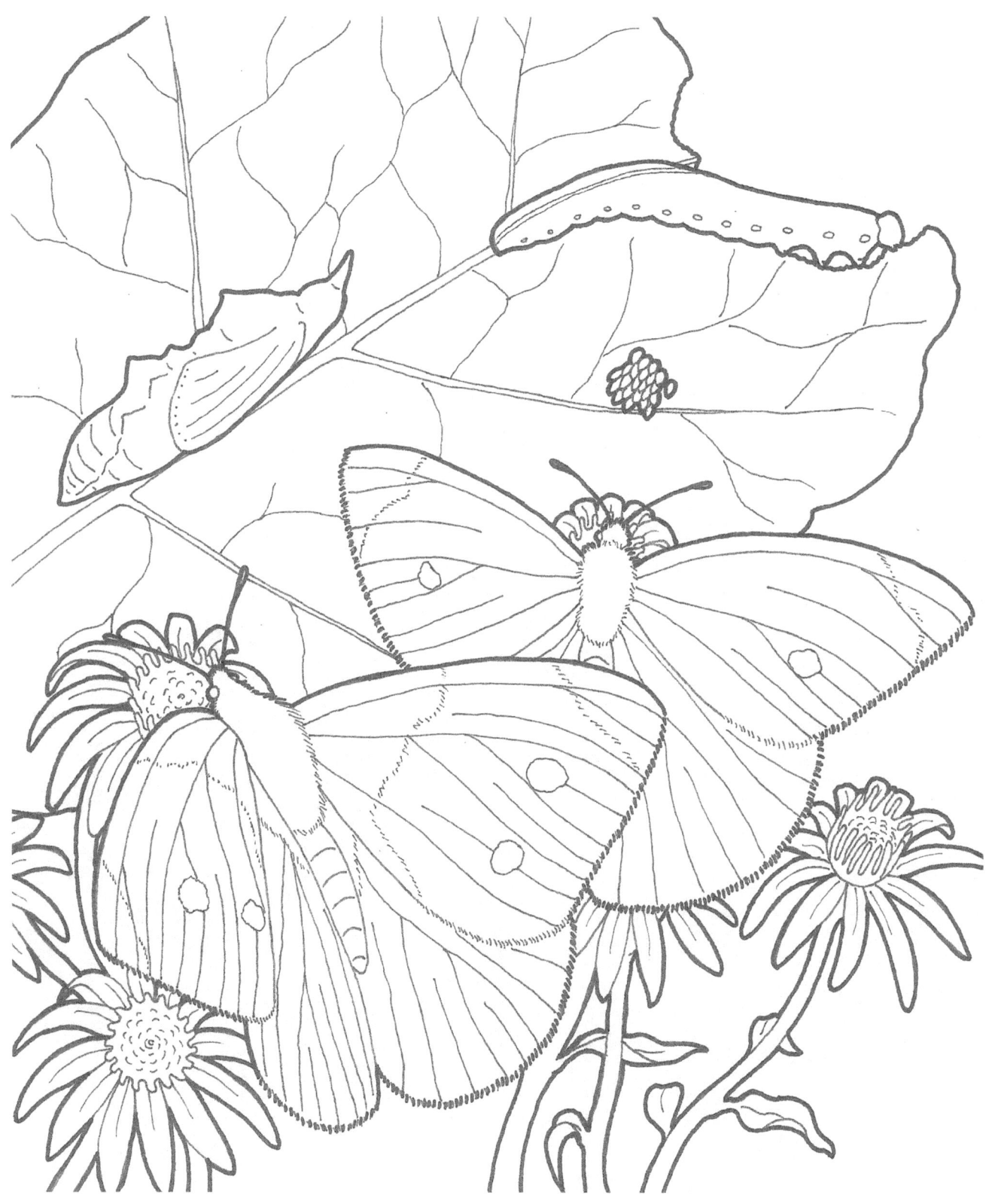

Cabbage White

Females have two black spots on the upper wings, while males have only one. In
true nature to their name, the caterpillars feed on cabbage and other related plant
species.

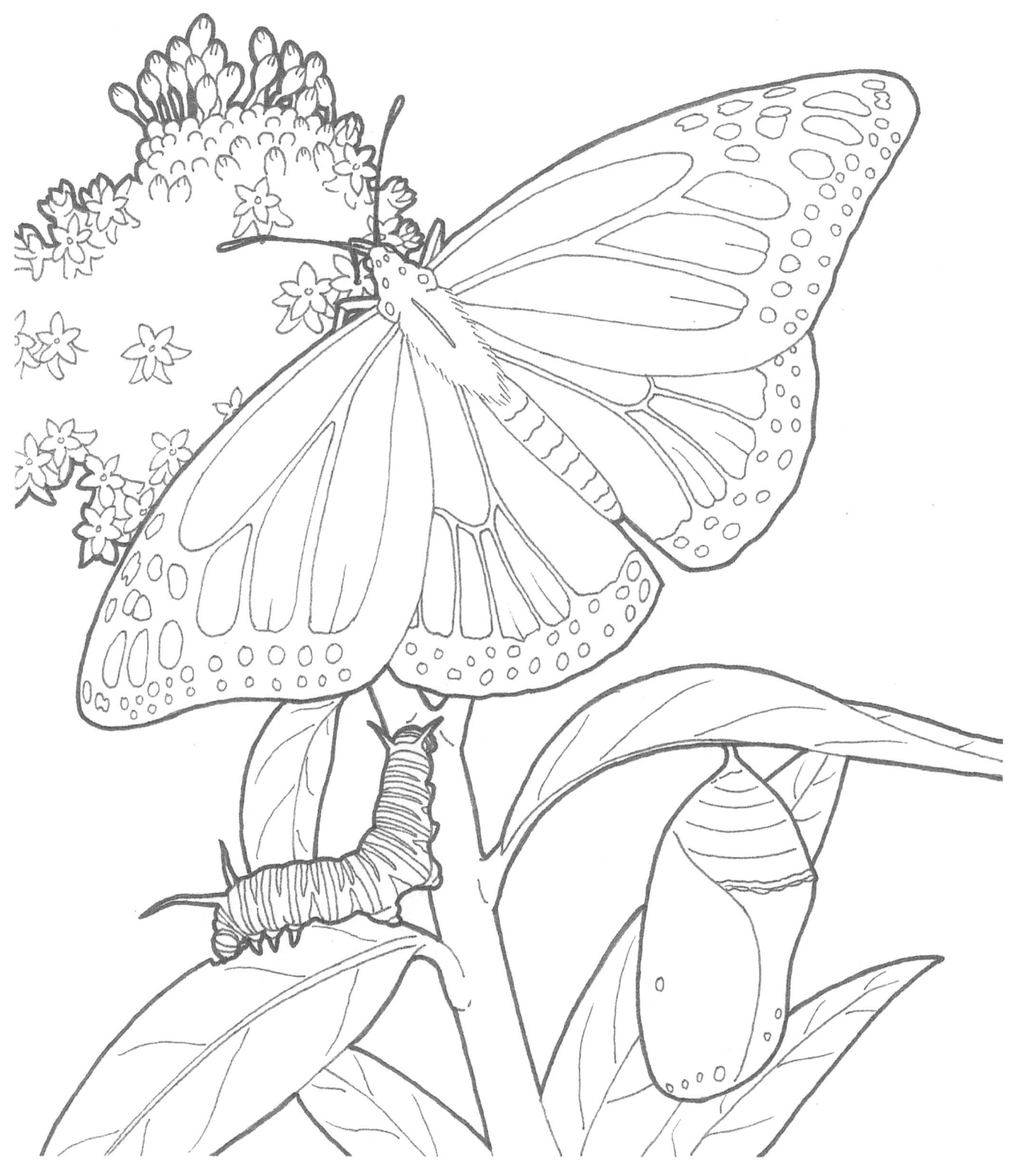

Monarch Butterfly

The monarch has one of the longest wintering migrations of any insect. They are an iconic and popular species, but the caterpillars will only feed on milkweed plants. So their abundance relies on the abundance of milkweed.

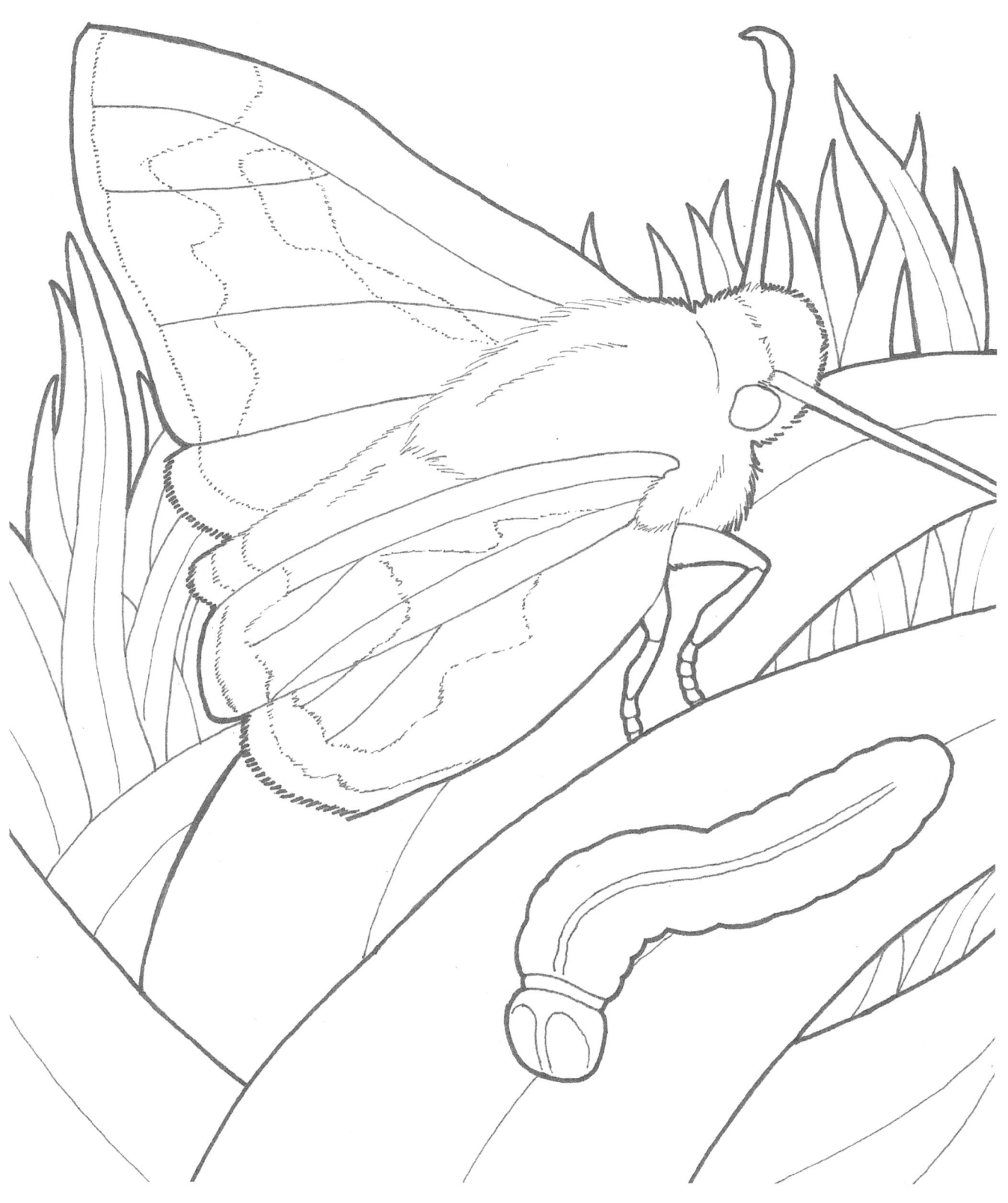

Woodland Skipper

Skippers are small relatives of butterflies with stocky builds and a hooked shape at the end of their antennae. The caterpillars feed on grass.

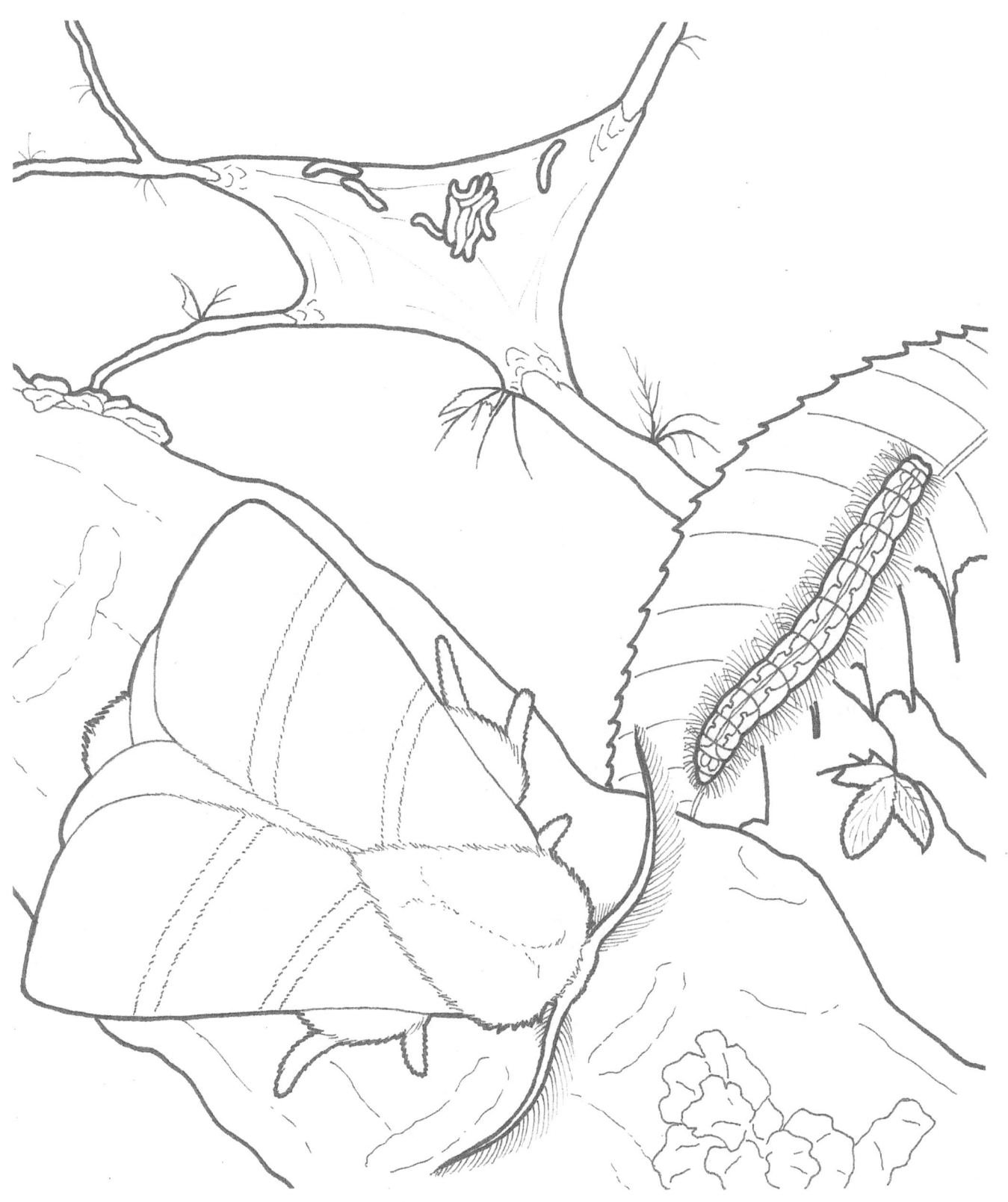

Tent Caterpillar

Unlike most species here, these caterpillars spin large silk nests to live on until they are large enough to go out foraging alone. They prefer fruit trees, and can be quite a pest when conditions are right. The adults are moths.

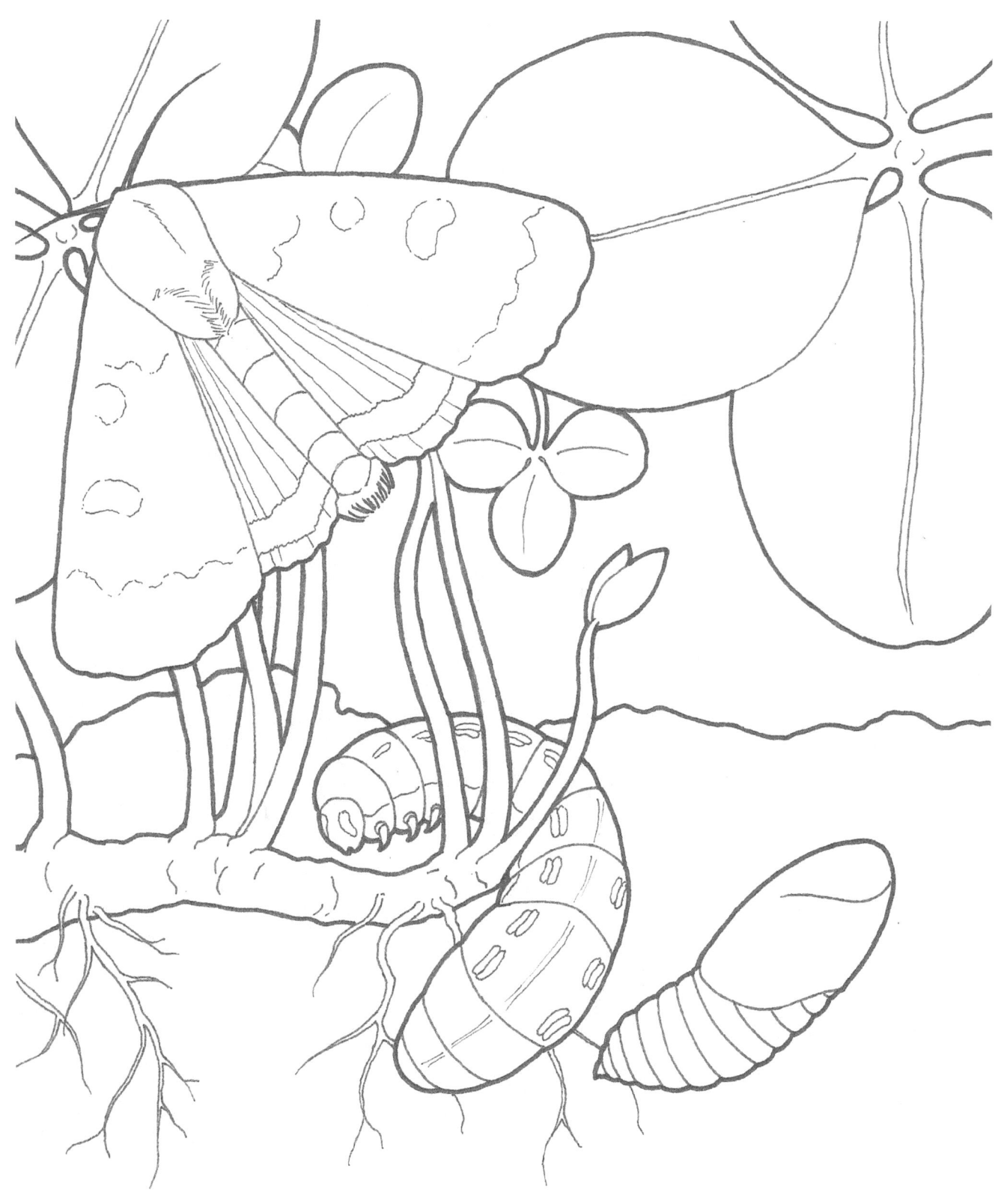

Yellow Underwing

Yellow underwings are large moths whose larvae eat the roots of many popular garden plants such as clover, strawberries, potatoes, and lettuce. Doing so can harm the plant, so they are often considered pests.

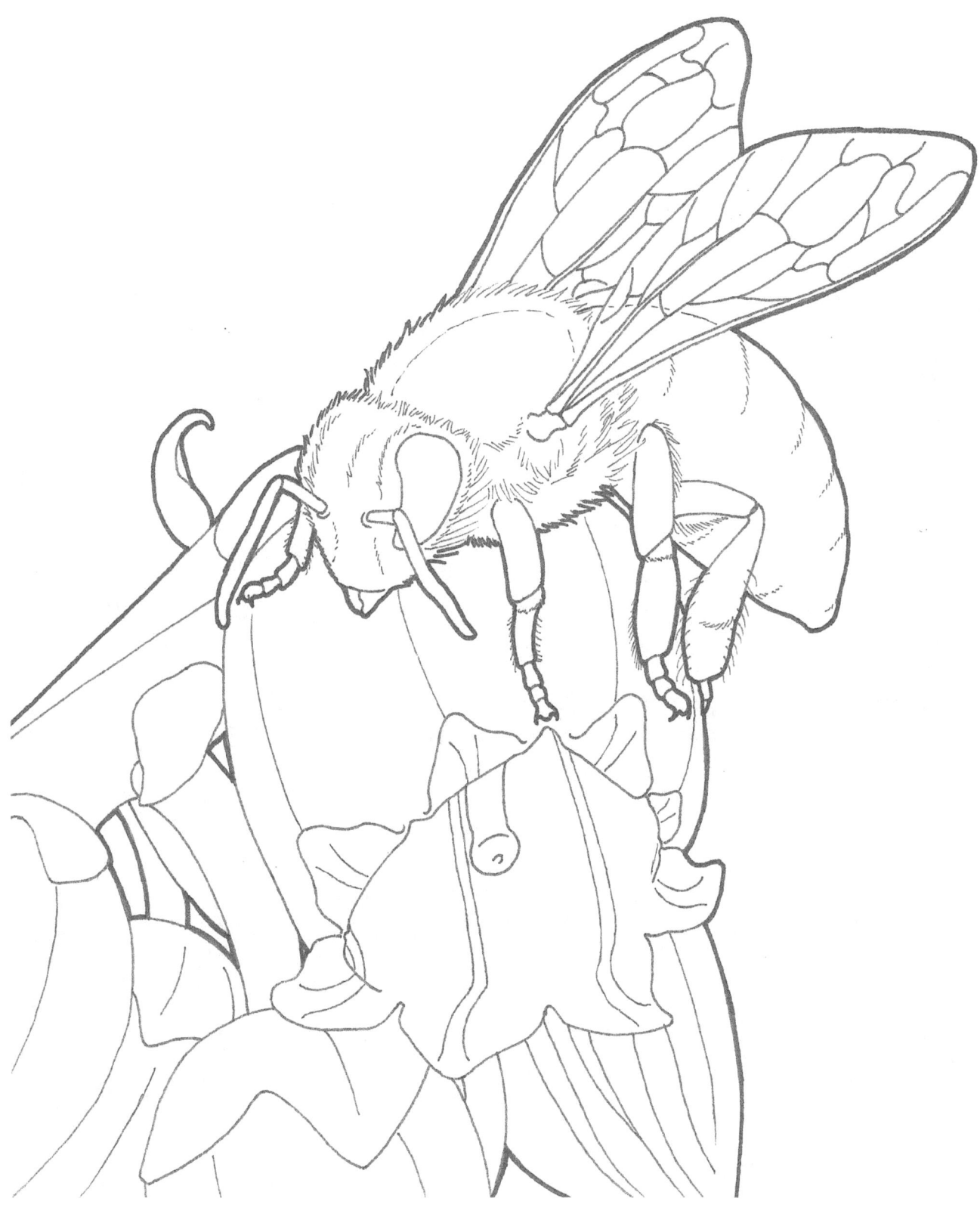

Honeybee

Honeybees are the most well known species of bee. They originated from Southeast Asia, but have been domesticated and spread to almost every major continent. They form the largest hives of any bee species, up to 60,000 bees!

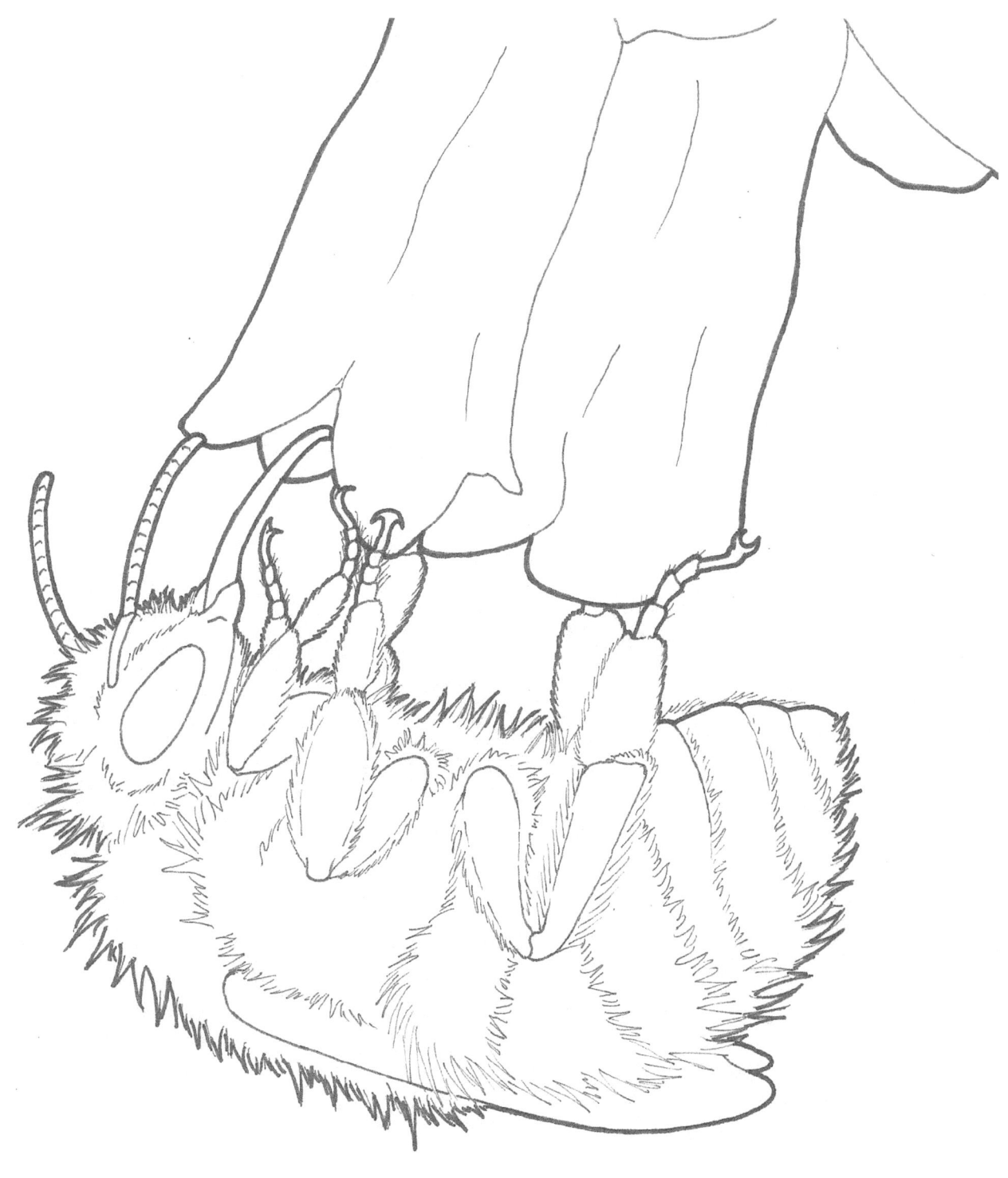

Bumble Bee

Bumble bees are the first bees to emerge in spring. Due to their size, covering of hair and the ability to warm up their flight muscles up to 30 degrees Celsius (86 degrees Fahrenheit) they can withstand colder temperatures than most other insects. They nest in small hives, usually in the ground, and are quite docile despite having stingers.

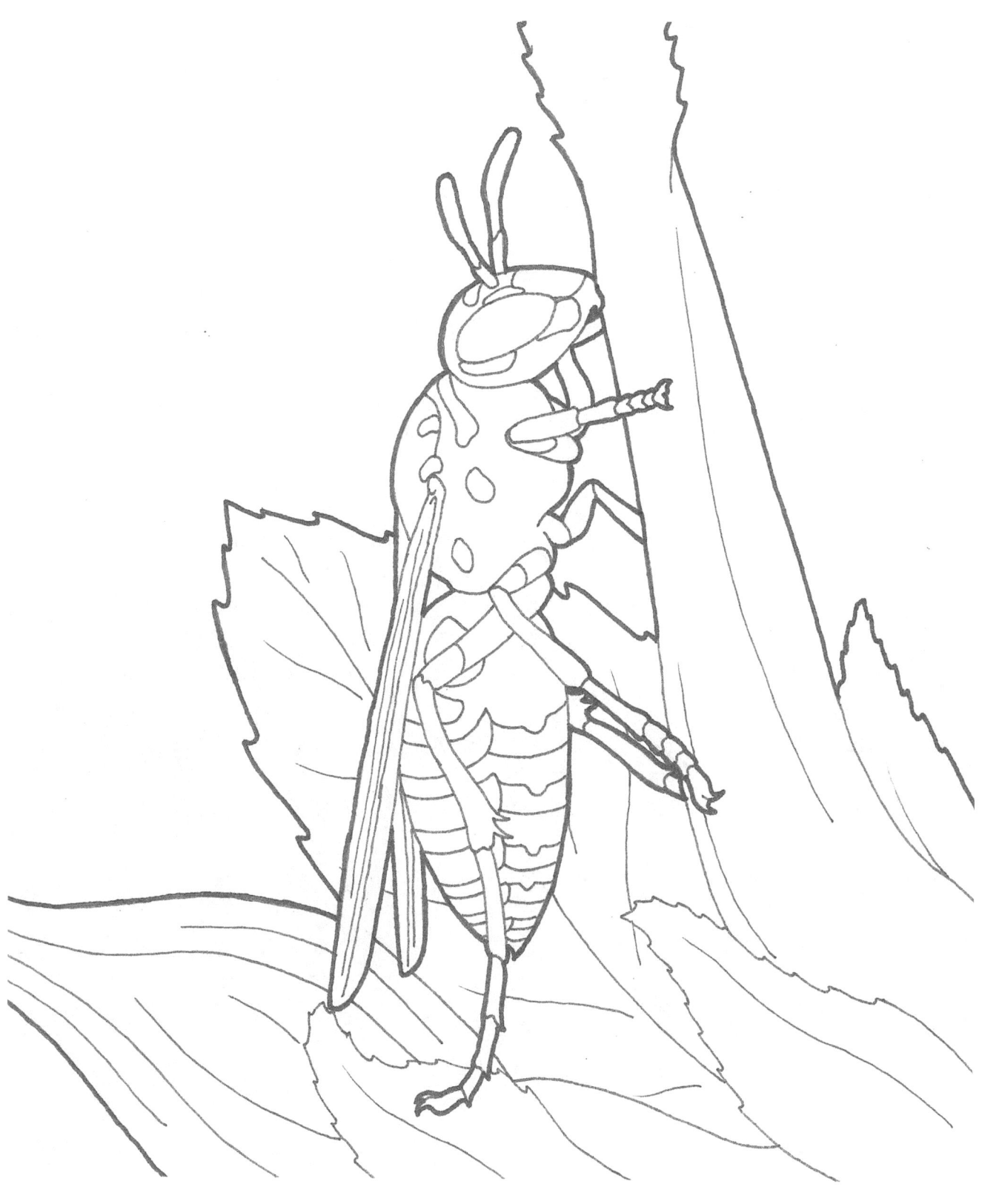

Paper Wasp

Paper wasps eat mostly caterpillars and are surprisingly docile for a wasp species. As their name suggests, they make their nests out of chewed up wood. They have yellow antenna, while yellow jackets have black antenna.

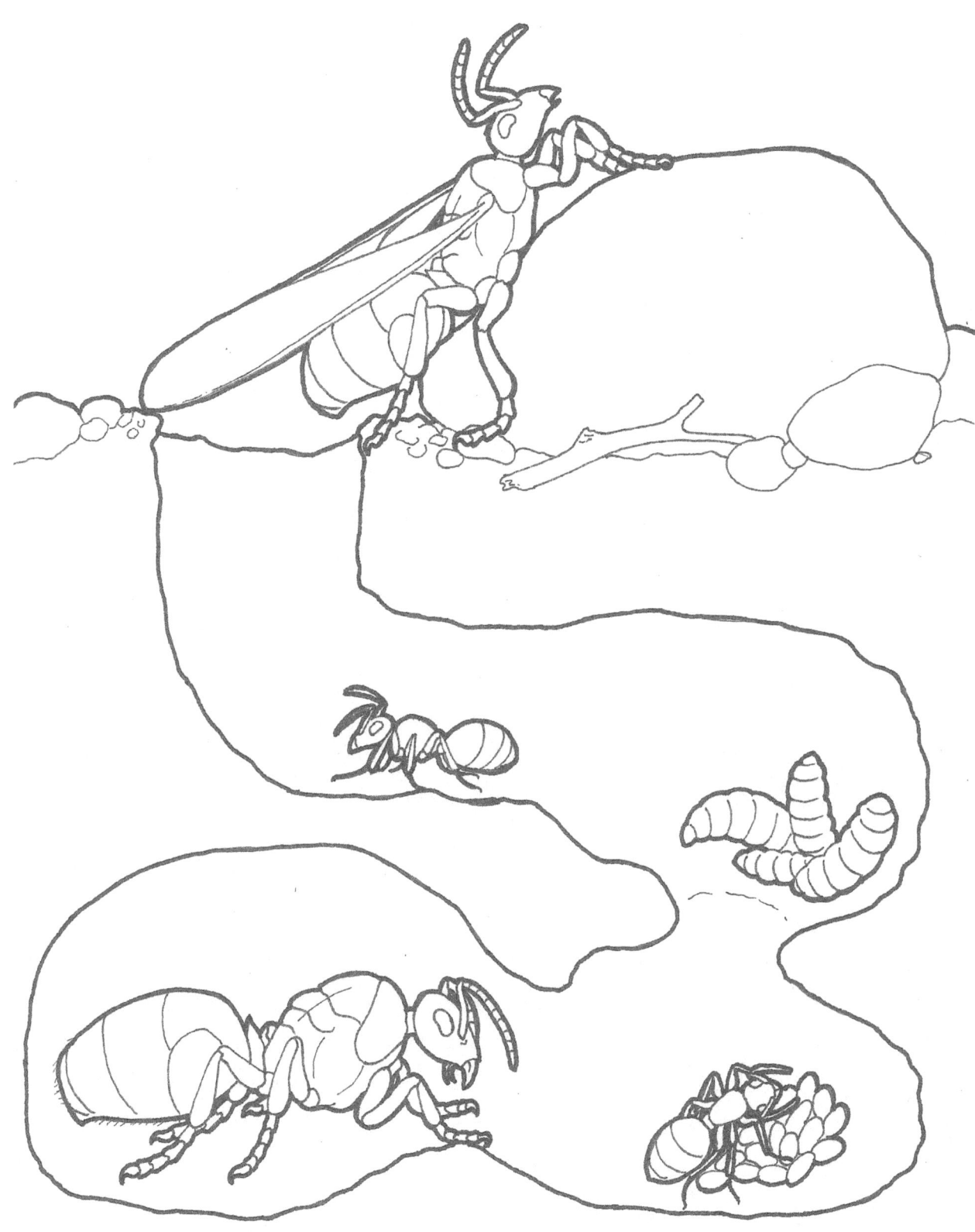

Ants

Ants live in colonies controlled by a queen. Workers are all female, and once a year the queen will produce winged males and females who fly off to start new colonies.

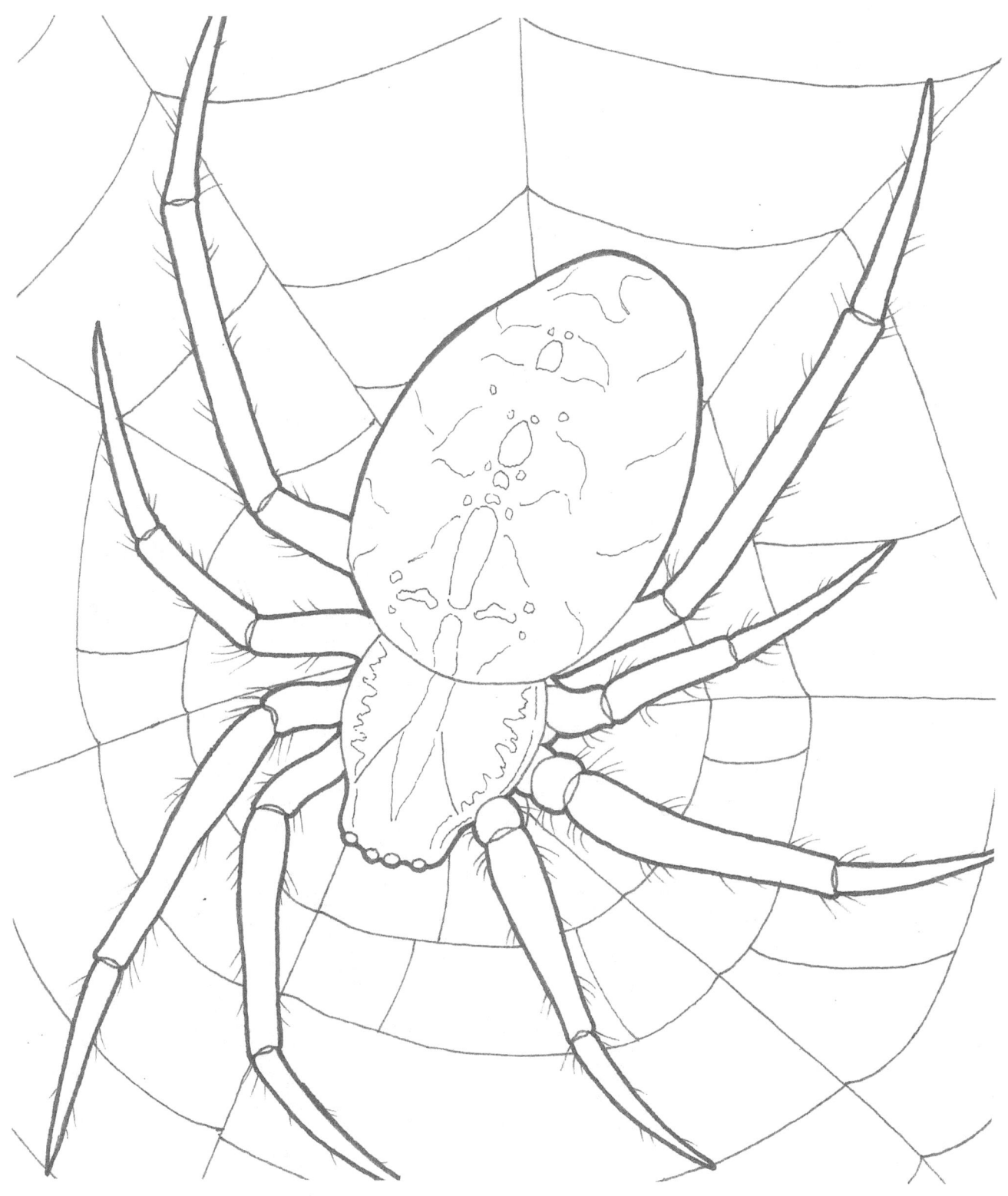

Orbweaver Spider

Unlike insects, spiders have two body segments, the cephalothorax and abdomen. The eight legs are all connected to the cephalothorax. Spiders are important predators, eating flies and other pests. Orbweavers spin beautiful webs in open spaces.

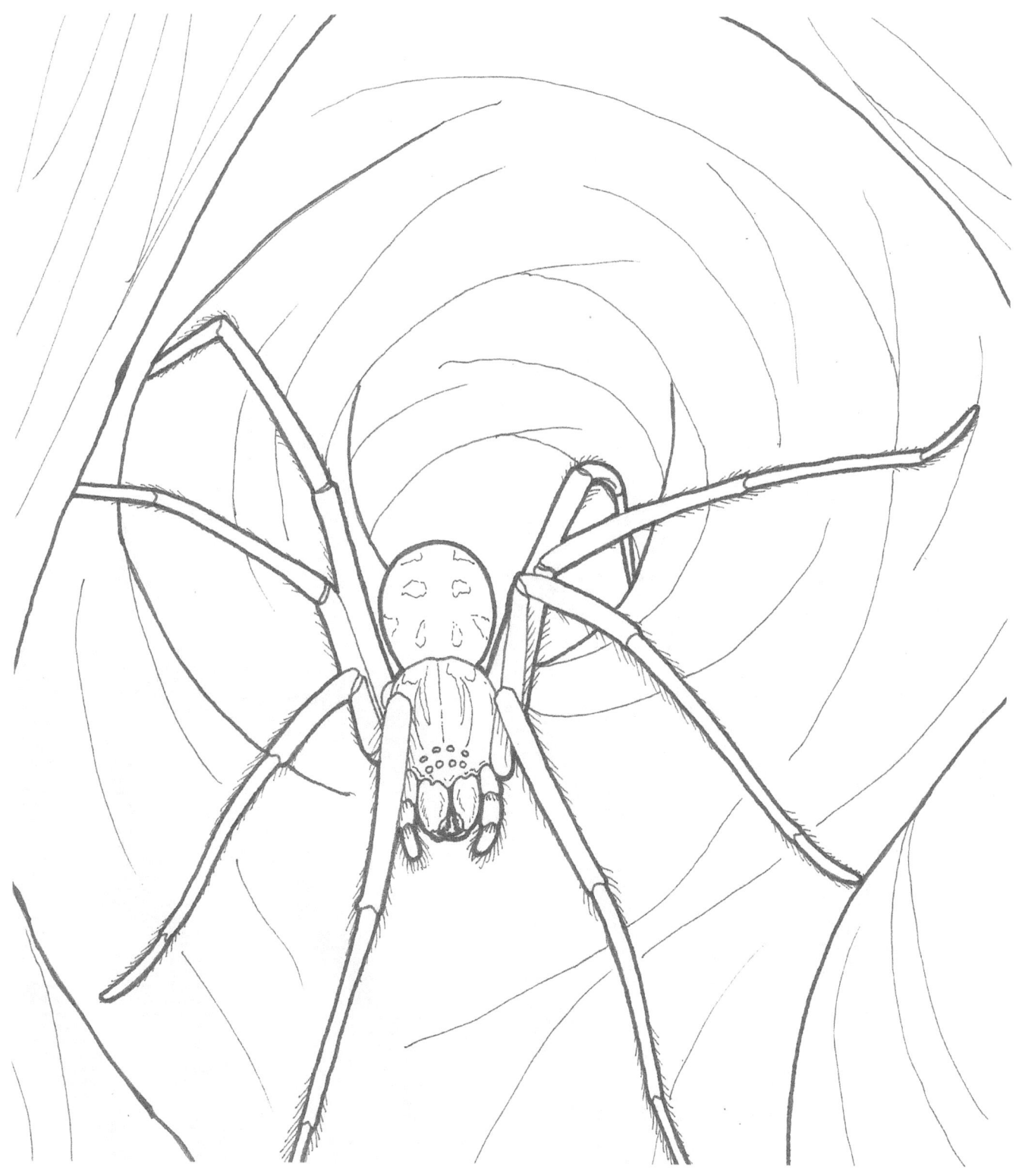

Giant House Spider

Originally from Europe, these large spiders are found living in buildings, usually in basements or dark corners. They hunt anything small that wanders into the area, including other spiders. Like most spiders, they have terrible eyesight. They are one of the fastest species of spider.

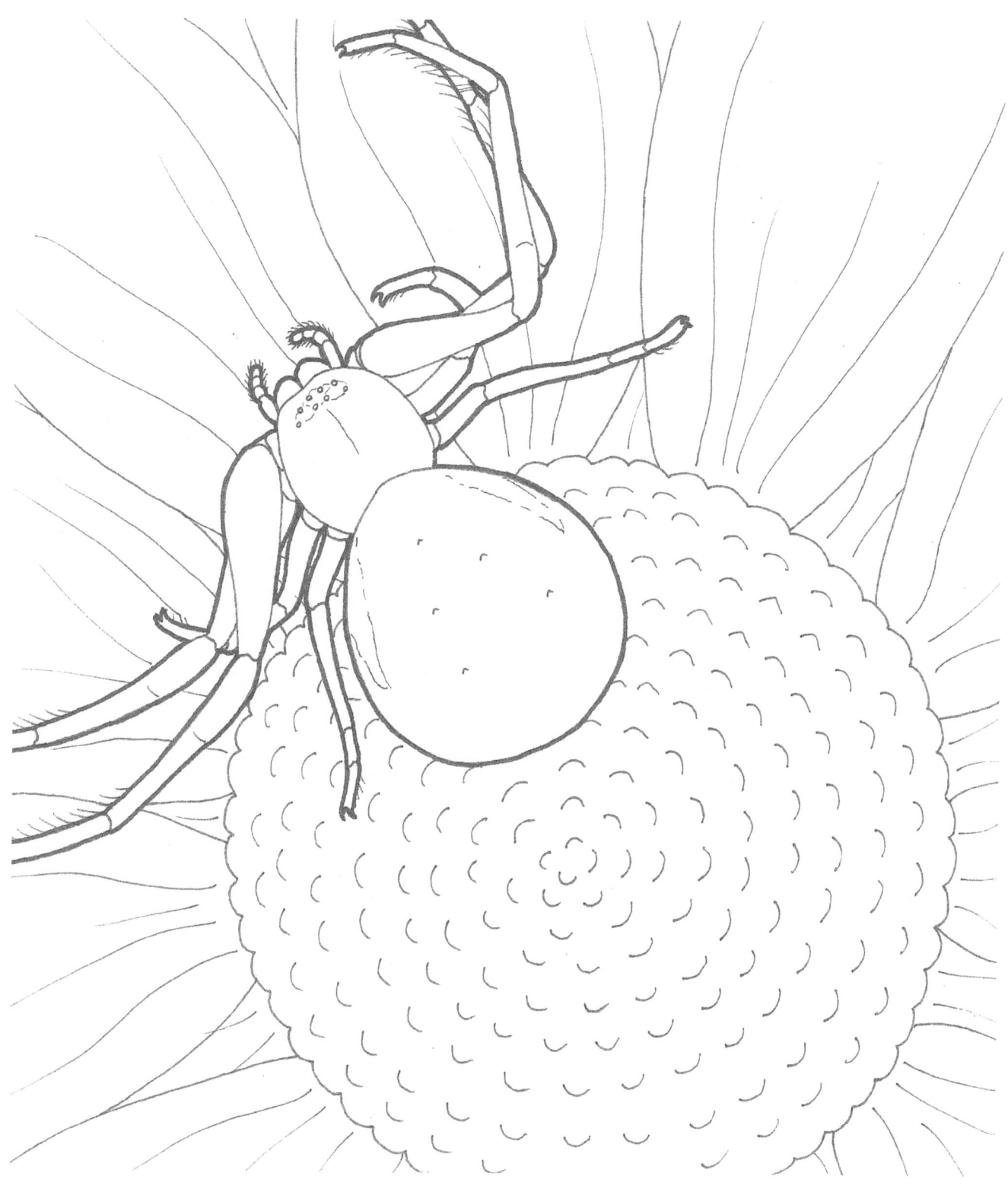

Crab Spider

Crab spiders are another type of spider that does not spin a web. Instead, they wait on a flower for a pollinating insect to come by then grab it with their strong front legs. The front legs have sharp spine-like hairs to grip prey. These spiders are harmless to humans, and can range in color from white to yellow.

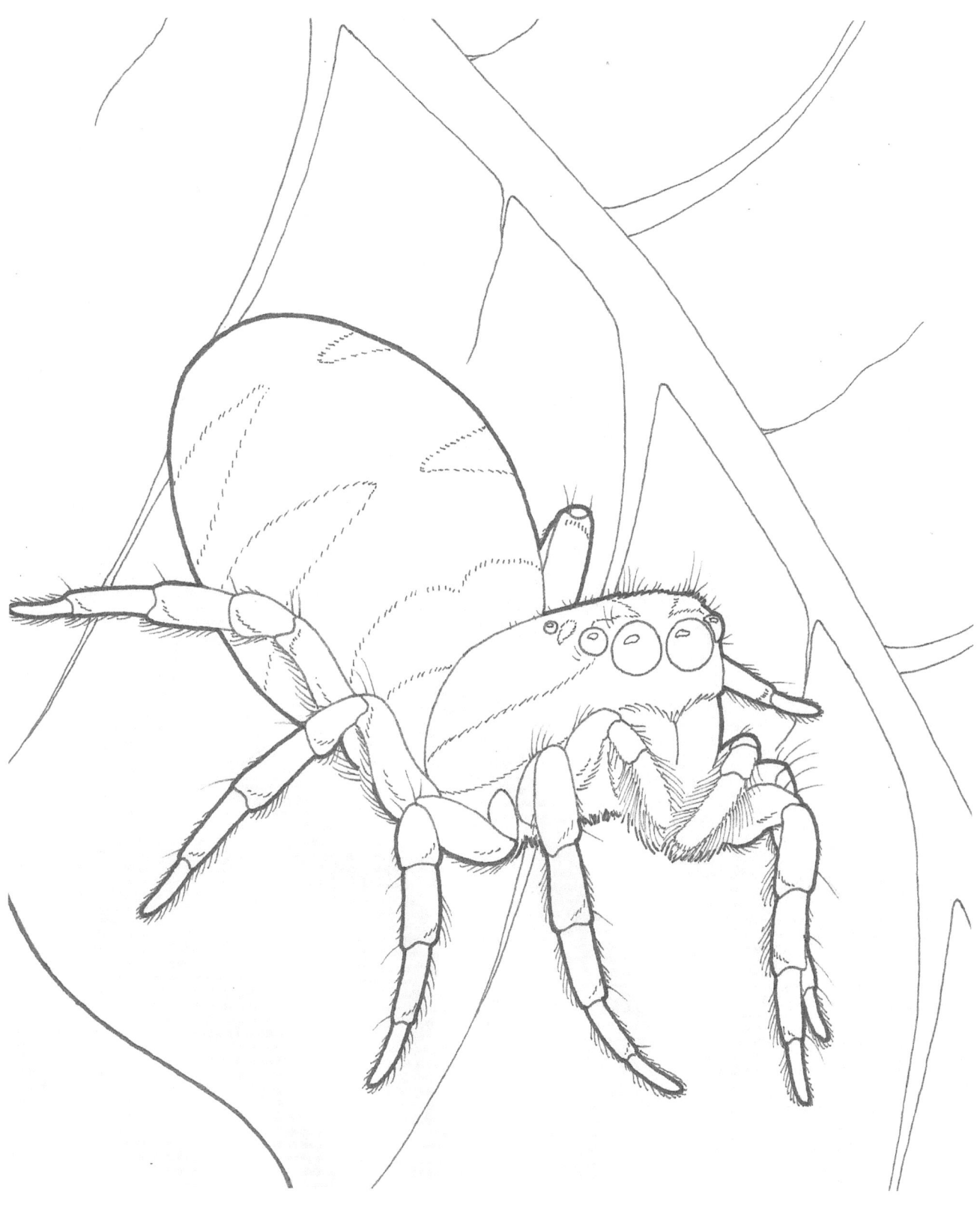

Jumping Spider

Jumping spiders have the best eyesight among spiders. They do not spin webs,
instead using strands as safety lines. These very small spiders are completely
harmless to humans.

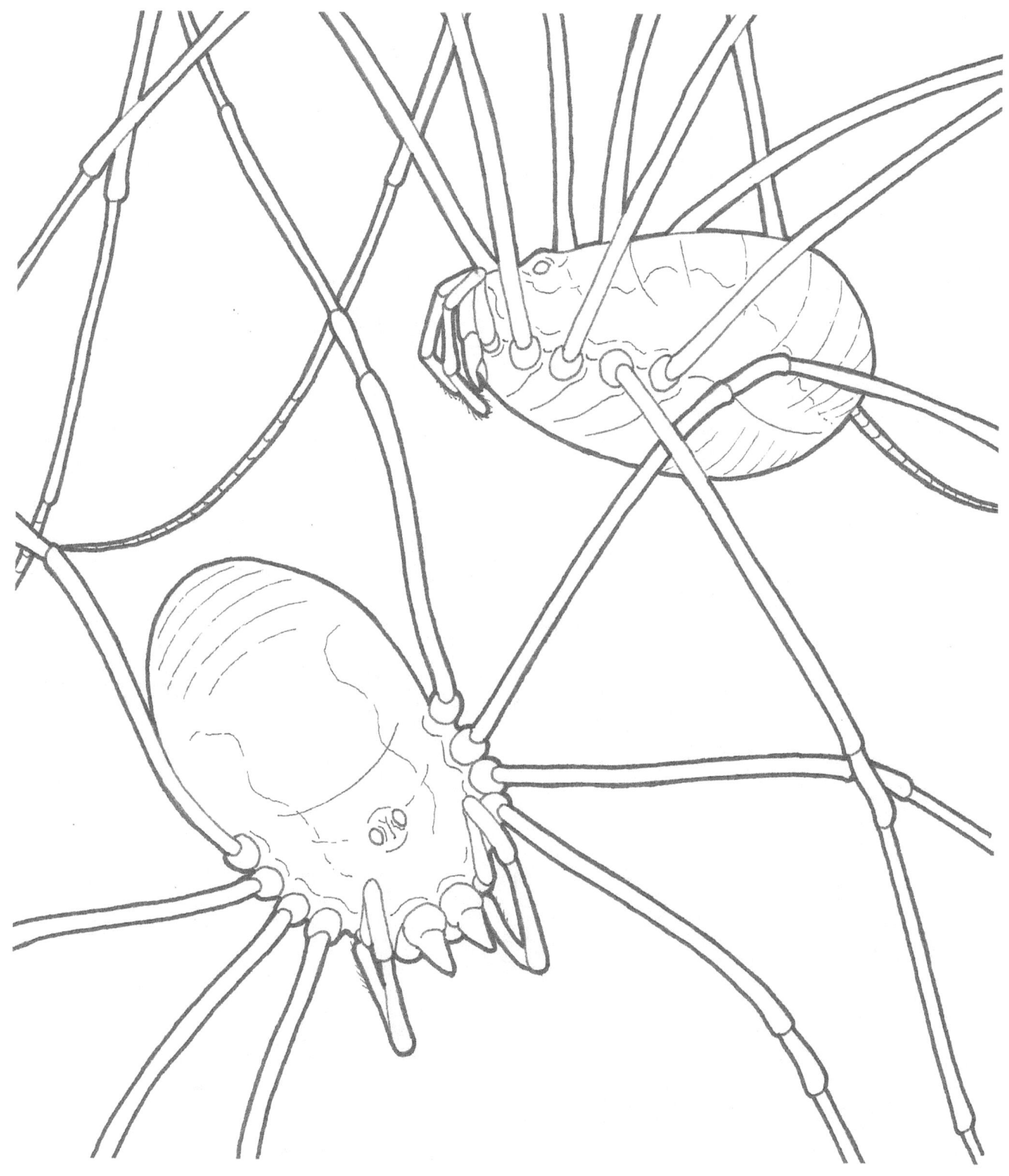

Harvestman

Also called daddy longlegs, these arachnids are only distantly related to spiders. They have small pinchers instead of fangs, and it is a common myth that they are highly venomous. Harvestmen hunt garden pests and are often found sunning themselves on fences.

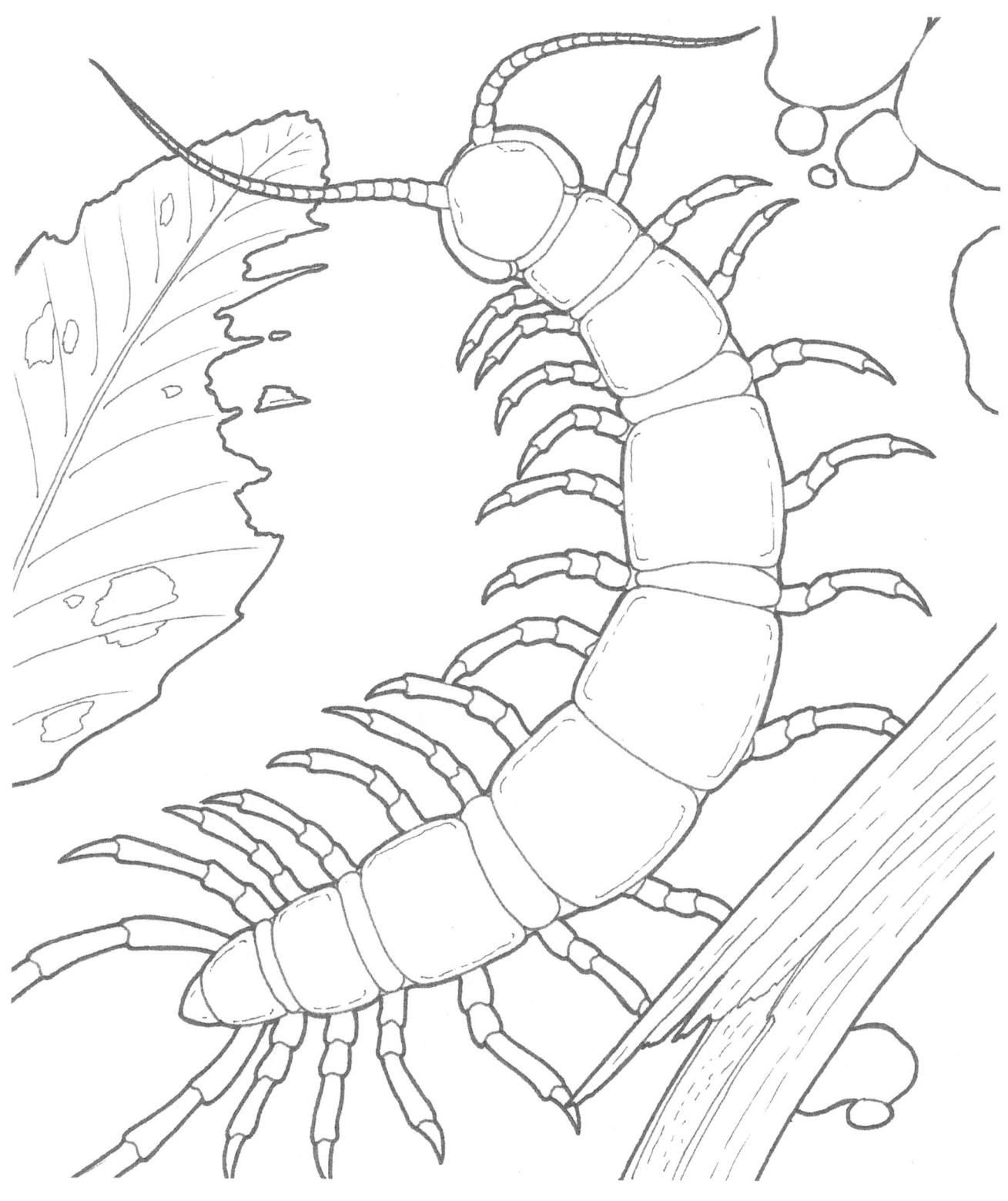

Centipede

Centipedes are voracious predators, hunting any small invertebrates they come across, making them a handy species to have in the garden. They are characterized by having only one set of legs per body segment and a large set of jaws. Careful, they can bite.

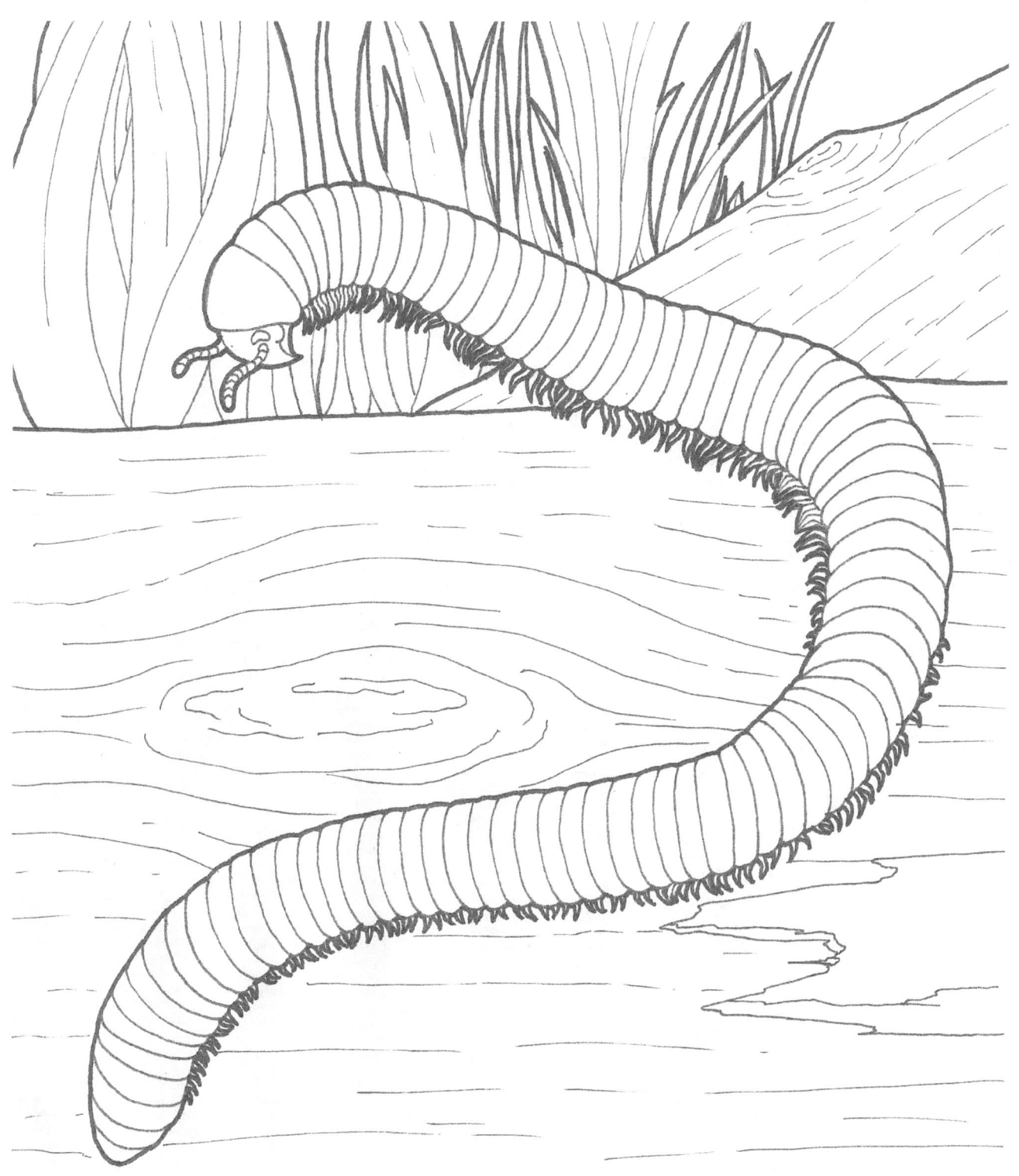

Millipede

Often mistaken for centipedes, millipedes are quite different. They have two sets of legs for every body segment, and are herbivores. Millipedes are important composters in the ecosystem. Often found under logs or in compost heaps, they are completely harmless.

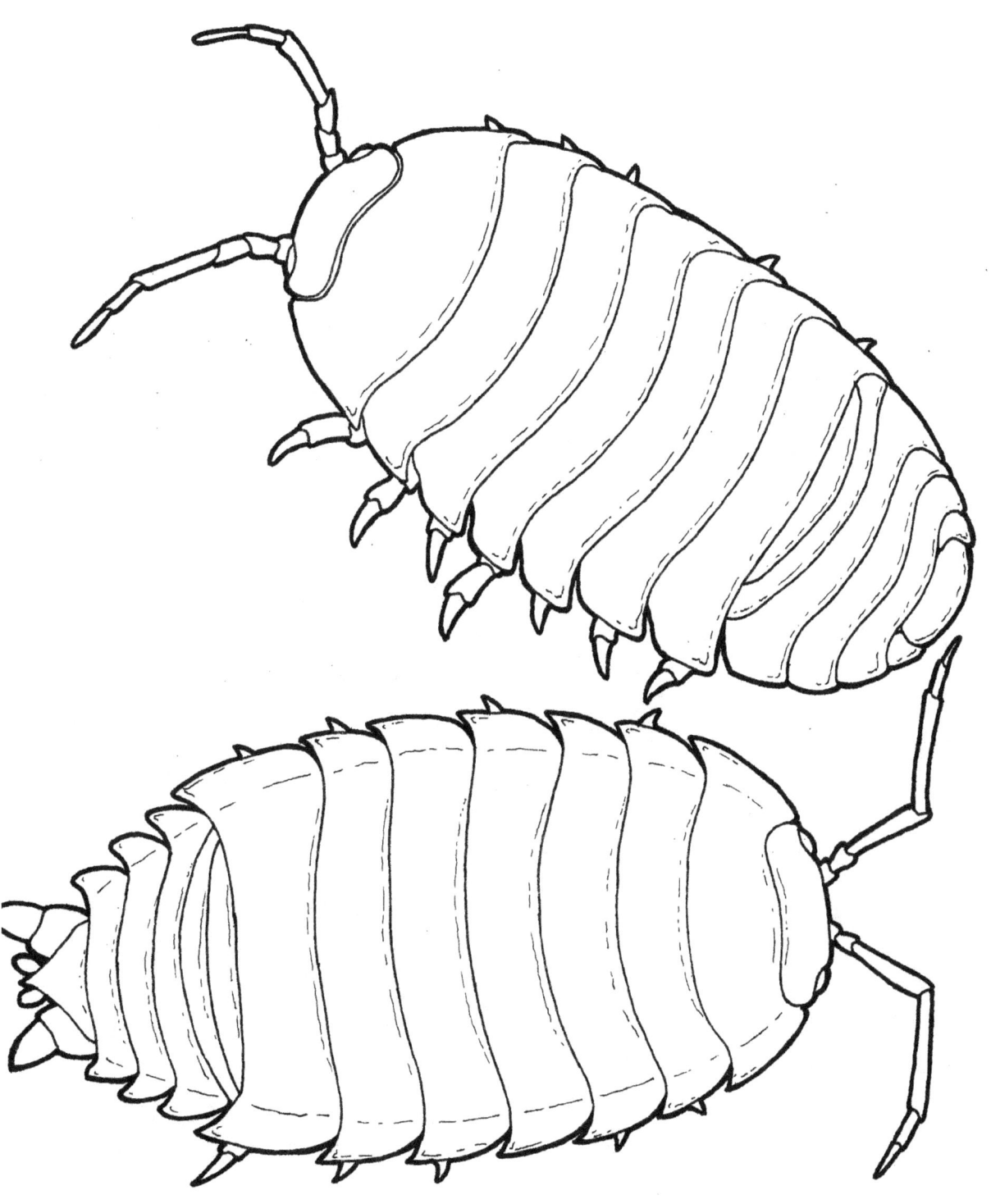

Pillbug & Sowbug

Though they are often called the same names interchangeably, pillbugs and
sowbugs are distinctly different. Pillbugs are able to completely curl into a ball for
defense, while sowbugs cannot. Both serve as important decomposers, consuming
rotting plant matter such as old logs.

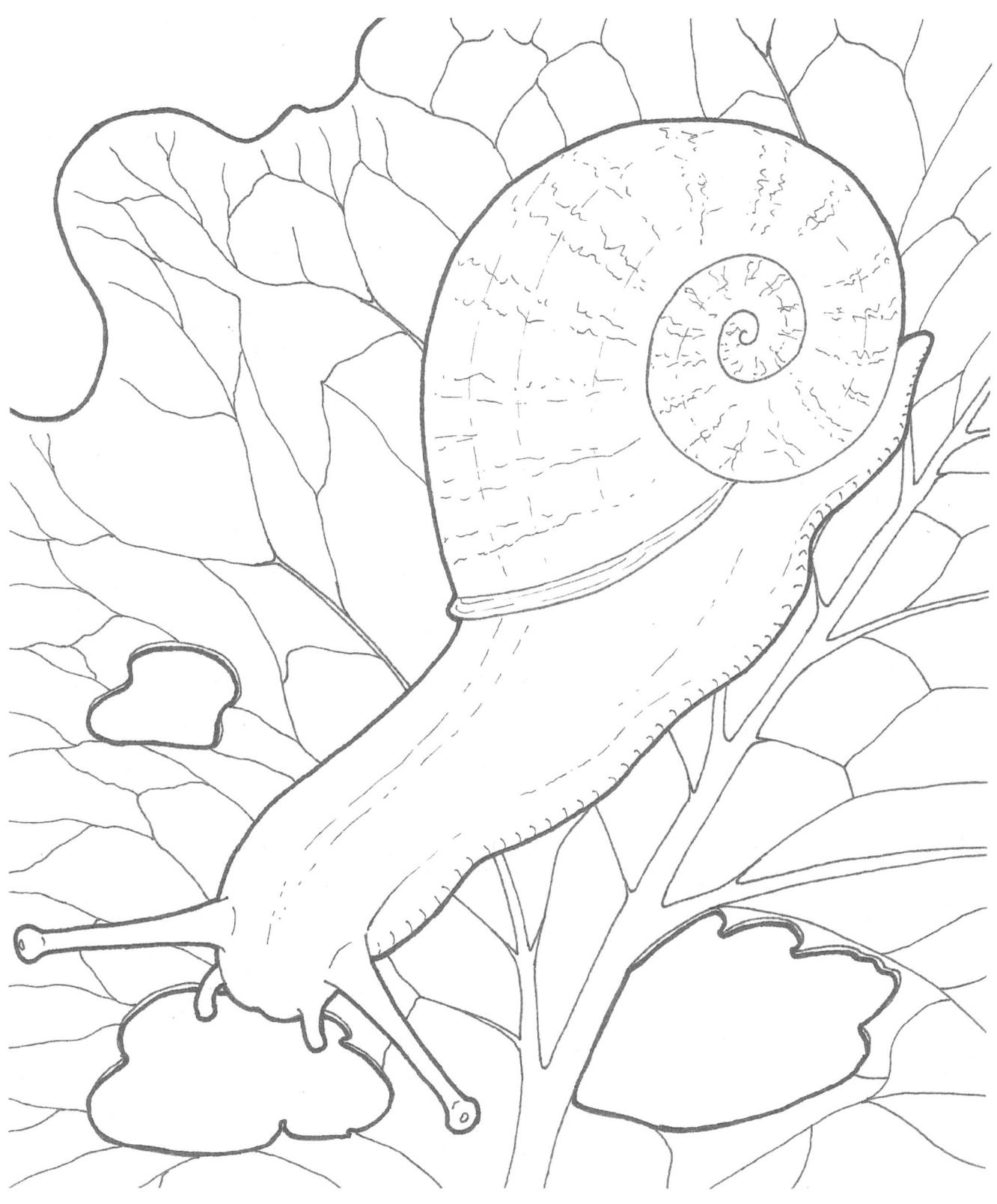

Garden Snail

Originally from Europe, these large snails are common in gardens and parks. They are considered invasive pests as they eat many popular garden plants, reproduce fast, and have few predators.

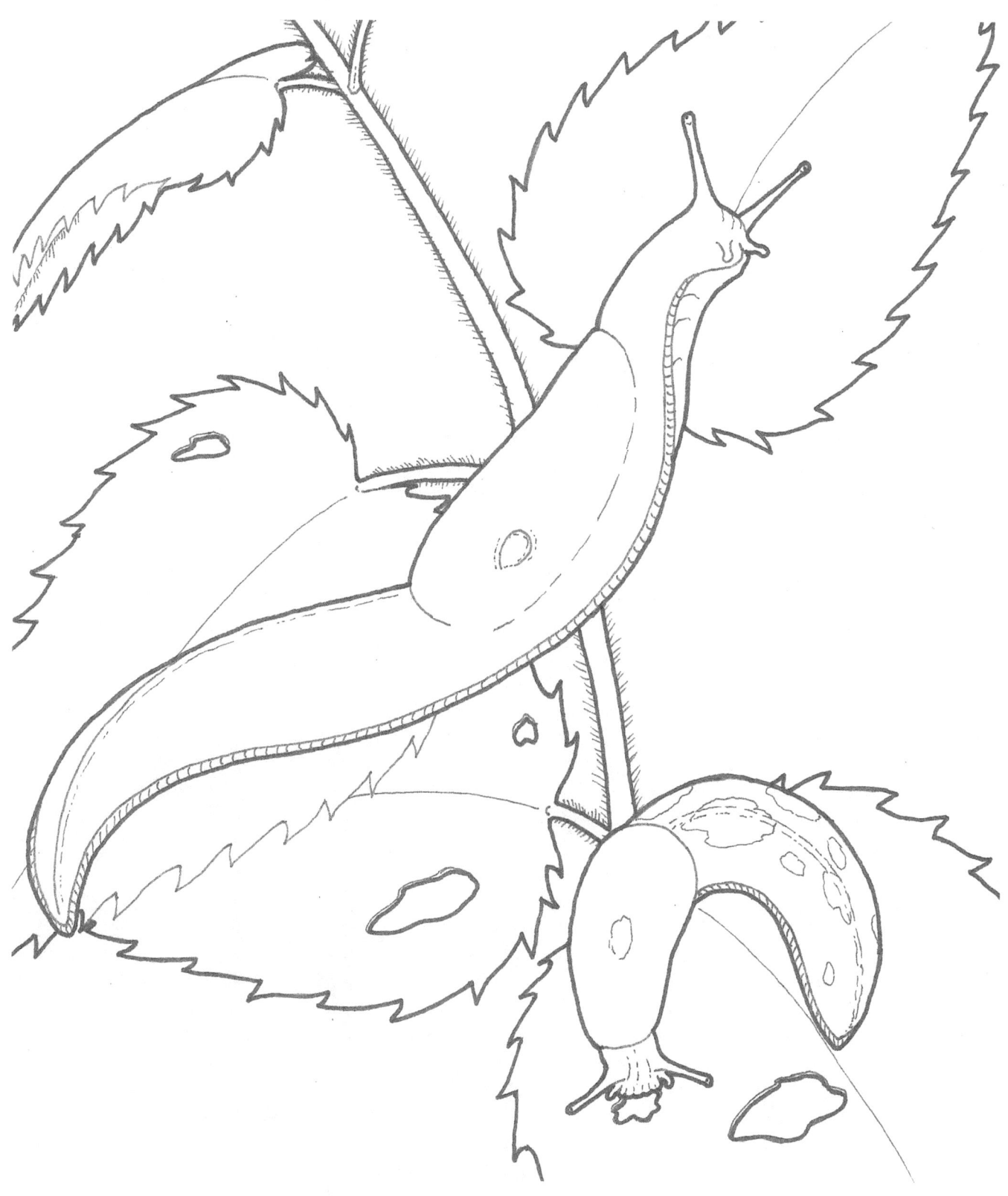

Banana Slug

As the second largest land slug in the world, banana slugs are easy to spot in their forest habitats. They eat both live plants and decomposing plant matter. They come in a variety of shades of yellow as well as yellow with dark brown spots.

www.ingramcontent.com/pod-product-compliance
Lightning Source LLC
Chambersburg PA
CBHW081206180526
45170CB00006B/2239